Multicultural Societies
in
Conflict and Coexistence

Proceedings of the Fifth Rotary International District 5300
Peace Conference

Edited by
R. Hrair Dekmejian
University of Southern California

Multicultural Societies
in Conflict and Coexistence

Published by Rotary Club of La Verne, California. 1999

Major funding for this publication was provided by The Rotary Foundation.

Multicultural Societies in Conflict and Coexistence

TABLE OF CONTENTS

FOREWORD

The quest for a world of peace, goodwill and mutual understanding represents the very essence of Rotary's global message and mission. Yet, as we prepare for the next century, we are faced with the growing specter of interethnic conflict and the challenge of building a world of multicultural concord and coexistence.

Through international service, every Rotarian has a unique opportunity to work to ensure a more peaceful and livable world. As individuals we are limited in what we can do alone. But by joining together with more than 1,200,000 Rotarians in some 160 countries and 35 geographical regions, we become part of a dynamic force united to serve all humankind in the cause of peace. This is the ultimate goal of Rotary International, and as Rotarians and citizens we are destined to make a difference in our communities and in the world.

The papers in this volume were presented at the Fifth Annual Rotary Peace Conference held on April 18, 1998 at the University La Verne. The conference was organized by the Rotary Club of La Verne under the auspices of Rotary International District 5300, with the generous support of The Rotary Foundation. Authored by distinguished academics, the papers explore the various dimensions of conflict and concord in multicultural communities in the United States and abroad. It is our hope that this monograph will contribute in a modest way to our understanding of the challenges we face in our quest to build a better world community.

Garbis Der Yeghian, Ph.D.
Governor 1999-2000
Rotary International District 5300

Editor's Preface

MULTICULTURAL SOCIETIES IN CONFLICT AND COEXISTENCE

The community of nations emerging from the Cold War has been faced with the pull of conflicting forces and movements, which have had a profound impact on national and international relations. The first of these is the powerful current of economic and cultural globalization led by the United States and other advanced industrial countries. As a transnational phenomenon, globalization has been increasingly challenged by the rise of multiculturalism – the quest for specific cultural, civilizational and/or ethnic identities, in the United States and abroad. Indeed, in the contemporary milieu of socioeconomic globalization, individuals and social groups are beset by a pervasive sense of identity crisis, which has prompted a return to their former psychosocial anchors and a reaffirmation of eroding civilizational, cultural and/or ethnic identities.

Although the current trend toward multiculturalism represents a reaction to the sweeping force of globalization, its deeper roots are to be found in the formative history of the modern nation-state system. The emergence of the first nation-states in Europe, and the subsequent expansion of nation statism to the newly independent countries of the Third World, were based on the imposition of homogenizing ideologies, which sought to deemphasize or even erase sub-national cultural and ethnic identities in the name of a single all-encompassing national identity. The breakup of empires after World War I and President Woodrow Wilson's call for self-determination, brought a renewed focus on ethno-national identities. The civil rights movement in the United States, and the waves of immigration of the 1980s and 1990s, pushed the problem of multiculturalism to the forefront of American public discourse. Meanwhile, the demise of the Soviet Union and the end of the Cold War unleashed numerous interethnic conflicts and migrations, which prompted Russia and the European countries to focus on the problem of inter-cultural conflict resolution and modalities of multicultural coexistence. At the 20th Century's end, multiculturalism has become a worldwide concern, as well as a key factor in shaping U.S. domestic politics and foreign policy.

The development of distinct social identities has been a persistent feature in history's evolution. Despite the pull of countervailing forces, human diversity remains a fact of life in the mosaic of today's global village, defined by one or several social boundaries, i.e., language, religion, race, kinship, tribe, region, nation, gender, class, civilization and collective historical experience. In view of the prevalence of multiple group identities in most of today's nation-states, the challenge of political leadership is to create the conditions to ameliorate conflict and promote coexistence in multicultural societies.

The collection of papers in this volume, presented at the 8th Annual Rotary International Peace Conference at the University of La Verne on April 18, 1998, examine aspects of multiculturalism in the United States, Canada, Mexico and several European and Third World countries. The common themes addressed by the authors of these case studies are the identification of the factors which produce conflict in multicultural societies and the factors which promote inter-communal peace and coexistence. In their totality, these scholarly papers offer readers an appreciation of the social and political complexities of the human condition, and the challenges awaiting humankind at the dawn of the 21st Century.

R. Hrair Dekmejian, Ph.D.
Professor of Political Science
University of Southern California

CHAPTER I

MULTICULTURALISM IN CANADA
Alison Dundes Renteln, Ph.D.*

This essay offers an analysis of the policy of multiculturalism in Canada, one of three countries which are officially multi-cultural (the other two are Australia and Sweden).[1] Multiculturalism is interpreted in various ways, but I use it to refer to a policy which promotes respect for different cultures or ways of life. Various institutions promote this policy including governments and universities. Generally speaking, multi-culturalism refers to immigrant groups referred to as ethnic minorities, but it sometimes includes indigenous peoples as well.

The debate about multiculturalism in Canada uses slightly different vocabulary from terminology in the U.S. The Canadian lexicon includes, for instance, First Nations peoples and bands as terms for their indigenous groups in contrast to the United States terminology of Native Americans, Indians, or tribes. Canadians also make reference to "visible minorities" for people of color.

Canada offers a useful contrast for the comparative analy-sis of multiculturalism policies.[2] Canada's experience with multiculturalism is generally regarded as "a resounding suc-cess."[3] The metaphor of the mosaic is used in contrast to the melting pot of the U.S. which means that ostensibly Canada supports the model of cultural pluralism in contrast to the model of forced assimilation.[4] Additional evidence that cultur-al rights are taken more seriously in Canada is the fact that the scholars most famous for advocating the right to culture are Canadians, e.g., Will Kymlicka, the author of *Multicultural Citizenship*.[5]

* Alison Dundes Renteln is Associate Professor of Political Science, University of Southern California. She holds a Ph.D. from the University of California, Berkeley.

5

But what is the status of multiculturalism in Canada? Though Canada is relatively more pro multiculturalism than the U.S., it is not as supportive of this policy as is commonly believed.[6] In order to see what lies behind Canadian multiculturalism, we need to consider the historical background of multiculturalism, the structure of government in Canada, and the implementation of selected public policies.

What we will see is that during the past twenty years Canada has experienced a backlash against multiculturalism.[7] Some writers call the policy "mosaic madness"[8] and "a cult of minorities."[9] Ultimately, then, as I will show, despite the appearance of support for multiculturalism, the policy has not been as successful as many would lead us to believe.[10]

This is an important issue because Canada has struggled over establishing its national identity. Some argue that multiculturalism is part of Canada's national identity. Others would go so far as to say that multiculturalism is the key to Canadian national identity.[11] Hence the difficulties associated with this policy reveal a basic challenge to Canadian national identity.

Historical Background

Before the Europeans arrived, First Nations peoples were already living in Canada.[12] Although the European powers initially honored the treaties they negotiated with the First Nations, the decline of the First Nations' military power was accompanied by a change in government policy. Canada gradually intervened to a greater extent, eventually adopting a policy of compulsory enfranchisement. The solution to the Indian problem was to ensure that they were "absorbed into Canadian society, by compulsion if necessary."[13]

Immigrants faced similar pressures to conform to Anglo standards. During the mid-nineteenth century many immigrants arrived in Canada only to emigrate later to the United States.[14] Indeed, for thirty years after confederation Canada's "most pressing problem" was the loss of tens of thousands of its population to the U.S. One scholar commented that: "The Americans may say with truth that if they do not annex Canada, they are annexing Canadians."[15] As a result of this phenomenon, Canada early on tried to preserve its existence as a nation-state by encouraging more immigrants to move to Canada.

Despite the need for more immigrants, the settlers were profoundly "Anglocentric."[16] In short, xenophobia characterized the attitudes of Canadians in the early period. For instance, although the French speaking population was crucial to "preventing the absorption of Canada into the U.S. during the American revolution,"[17] the English speaking Canadians were not supportive of French. There were attempts to destroy French speaking communities outside Quebec.[18]

Those who remained in Canada often lived in rural ethnic enclaves. It is believed that this pattern of settlement laid the foundation for the so-called Canadian mosaic and subsequent adoption of the multiculturalism policy. Some of the historical accounts seem to suggest that it was largely an historical accident that Canada adopted the pluralism idea.[19]

Because Canada was in desperate need of persons to work in the mines and on the railroad, Canada permitted a great influx of Chinese for these purposes.[20] Concern was expressed about "non-assimilable" elements, and many were concerned about how to "Canadianize" so many diverse persons.[21] Clearly, there was an expectation that the vast majority of immigrants should conform to Anglo standards.

After World War I, Canada and the United States both favored halting immigration from regions of the world considered less desirable. Whereas the U.S. adopted draconian quo-

7

tas, Canada established four ethnic categories: British; preferred (American and Northwest Europeans); nonpreferred (Central and Eastern Europeans), and restricted (Italians, Greeks, and Jews).[22]   Pressures for laborers, however, led Canada to disregard its new immigration policy.

Most of the immigrants in the 1950s and 1960s were Europeans.   The 1962 and 1966 amendments to the Immigration Act of 1952 removed the ethnic categories. Afterwards, there was a dramatic shift away from European immigration to what were euphemistically called "non-traditional" sources of immigrants from Asia, North Africa, Latin America, and the Caribbean.[23]   From then on Canada had increasingly high numbers of immigrants from Asia.[24]   During the 1980s and 1990s there was a steady increase in the number of immigrants, despite the fact that public opinion polls showed that Canadians were opposed to it.[25]

Incorporation of Multiculturalism in Policy and Governmental Structure

The federal nature of Canadian government, the existence of English speaking and French speaking populations, and the First Nations peoples have all contributed to support for a multiculturalism policy.[26]   Canada adopted multiculturalism as an official policy in 1971.[27]   This followed the publication of a report by the Royal Commission on Bilingualism and Biculturalism.[28] The Commission recommended finding ways to protect cultures in Canada.   It also said that immigrants should be "integrated" into one of two societies, English speaking, Anglophone, or French speaking, Francophone. The key point is that integration was not considered as synonymous with assimilation meaning "total absorption into another linguistic and cultural group."[29, 30]   However, the conceptual distinction does not appear to have influenced policy formulation and implementation.

The government decided to establish a policy of multiculturalism within a bilingual framework. This was contrary to the Commission's recommendation of multilingualism. It is noteworthy inasmuch as the preference for two European languages conveys a symbolic message about the value of other languages. If language is a crucial component of culture, then bilingualism contradicts the policy goal of multiculturalism.

The government policy included four methods of promoting multiculturalism:

> 1. It would seek to assist all Canadian cultural groups that had demonstrated a desire and effort to continue to develop a capacity to grow and contribute to Canada and were in clear need of assistance.
> 2. It would assist members of all cultural groups to overcome cultural barriers to full participation in Canadian society.
> 3. It would promote creative encounters and exchange among all Canadian cultural groups in the interest of national unity.
> 4. It would continue to assist immigrants in acquiring at least one of Canada's official languages in order to become full participants in Canadian society.[31]

Interestingly, no subject was provided for third language training.

The federal government established a Directorate for Multiculturalism under the Secretary of State. The government introduced two changes: 1) it recommended bilingualism rather than multilingualism, and 2) it promoted multiculturalism in the case of so-called "ethnic voluntarism," meaning only in those instances where members of a group express a desire to maintain their ethno-cultural heritage and can show a dire need for assistance.

Within the legal system, special guarantees for multiculturalism were established. The 1982 Canadian Charter of Rights and Freedoms contains several provisions concerning cultural rights such as:[32]

Article 15

Equal protection without discrimination based on race, national or ethnic origin, colour, religion, sex, age or mental or physical disability.

Article 16

English and French are the official languages of Canada and have equality of status and equal rights and privileges as to their use in all institutions of the Parliament and government of Canada.

Article 25

The guarantee in this Charter of certain rights and freedoms shall not be construed so as to abrogate or derogate from any aboriginal treaty or other rights or freedoms that pertain to the aboriginal peoples of Canada including 1) any rights or freedoms that have been recognized by the Royal Proclamation of October 7, 1793.

Article 27

This Charter shall be interpreted in a manner consistent with the preservation and enhancement of the multicultural heritage of Canadians.

With the arrival of larger numbers of new "non-traditional" immigrant groups, there was pressure to broaden the multiculturalism policy. This resulted in the 1988 Multiculturalism Act, which was a response to the changing ethnic composition in Canada. This Act has theoretically given force of law to principles of racial and cultural equality and marks the continuing presence of multiculturalism in Canadian society.

Having considered the historical background in Canada which gave rise to the policy of multiculturalism, I turn to a few specific policies to see if cultural rights have, in fact, been vindicated. Contrary to expectation, Canadian institutions have been somewhat reluctant to support multiculturalism.

Public Policies: Case Studies where Multiculturalism Policy is Tested

The Cultural Defense

One policy which would institutionalize the recognition of cultural differences is known as the cultural defense. Canada briefly considered establishing an official cultural defense,[33] but the Justice Minister Alan Rock quickly rejected the proposal.[34] Had it been adopted, it would have authorized the consideration of a defendant's cultural background in criminal cases. Despite the absence of a formal policy, the cultural defense is invoked in Canada. When there have been unofficial attempts to raise cultural defenses, the Canadian courts have not been inclined to accept the argument. Two examples should suffice to demonstrate this point.

The relevance of culture for a defense of provocation was the central issue in the Canadian case of *R. v. Ly* (1987). A Vietnamese refugee became suspicious that his common law wife was no longer faithful to him. When he confronted her about this initially, explaining that he felt he had lost face in the eyes of the community, he spoke of committing suicide which his wife supposedly encouraged him to do. He took some pills but was treated in a hospital and survived. On one particular night he expected his wife home early and when she returned at two o'clock in the morning, he questioned her again. After she told him that where she had been was none of his business, he strangled her and tried again to kill himself.

At the trial he tried to emphasize the cultural significance of his wife's conduct, testifying that: "...his wife's infidelity had caused him to lose 'face', and 'honour', and this had a special importance to him because of his Vietnamese upbringing."[35] The chairman of a Vietnamese refugee association corroborated the cultural argument. But the trial judge's instruction to the jury on provocation diminished the power of the cultural argument.

According to the Criminal Code of Canada, to reduce a murder charge to manslaughter requires passing a two-pronged test. First, there must be a determination that the wrongful act or insult was of such a nature that it would deprive an ordinary person of self-control. Second, the accused must have reacted to the provocation, promptly before there was time for his passion to cool. The rationale for combining an "objective" reasonable man test and a "subjective" test of actual provocation is that an ordinary person might be provoked by something even though the accused was not (and vice versa).

The crux of the appeal was based on the trial judge's instruction that the jury not consider culture in assessing the first part of the test, namely whether the "ordinary person" would have been sufficiently provoked. As far as the judge was concerned, culture only goes to the question of whether the accused was actually provoked. But the defendant contended that the insult "could only be properly measured against the cultural background of the appellant."[36] As the jury did not evaluate the reaction of an average Vietnamese male, Ly was convicted of second degree murder. The three judges of the British Columbia Court of Appeal affirmed the decision of the lower court.[37]

Until the Canadian judiciary clarifies the nature of the test for provocation, the relevance of cultural arguments will be ambiguous. In *R. v. Ly* the judges followed precedent and took an unduly narrow view of provocation, one based almost exclusively on racial slurs. It is hard to fathom their reasoning.

It is also curious that American and Canadian appellate courts came to diametrically opposed conclusions in similar cases within a year of each other. In *People v. Aphaylath*[38] the court of last resort in New York (the state's Supreme Court) in a strikingly similar case, held that it was a reversible error to exclude evidence about the defendant's cultural background.

Another case in which a cultural defense was used, this time through a religious freedom defense, is the Canadian Supreme Court case of *Jack and Charlie v. R.* (1985). Two members of the Coast Salish Indian people were charged with violating a provincial Wildlife Act by hunting and killing a deer out of season. The reason for the hunt was the need to burn deer meat as part of a religious ceremony. An anthropologist explained the significance of the practice to the court:

> This is a very ancient traditional practice among all Coast Salish people and the essence of the ceremony is to provide food for a deceased relatives by burning it and the essence of the food, as I understand it, is transmitted through the smoke to the essence of the deceased person.[39]

> Failure to burn deer meat, as is required, may result in some form of divine retribution.[40]

The court dismissed the appeal for two reasons. The first was that: "The prohibition of hunting deer out of season by the Wildlife Act does not raise a question of religious freedom or aboriginal religion."[41] The peculiar reasoning was that the killing of the deer was not itself part of the religious ceremony and the Indians should have foreseen their religious need for deer meat and had frozen some for that purpose.[42]

Second, the Court objected to the idea that the reason why the defendants had violated the law should be deemed germane to the determination of their culpability. They agreed with the Crown that: "The intention of the Appellants that the deer meat be used for the burning ceremony was their 'ultimate intention' or 'motive'. As such, it is irrelevant to legal responsibility for the commission of the offence."[43]

If *R. v. Ly* and *Jack and Charlie v. R.* reflect the attitude of Canadian judges more generally, it appears that the Canadian judiciary is somewhat unwilling to extend the multiculturalism policy in the context of criminal cases involving either immigrants or First Nations peoples. Ironically, again a state supreme court in the United States in *State v. Berry*,[44] reached the opposite conclusion. It held that an Indian could raise a religious defense in a prosecution for failing to comply with hunting season policy.

Dress Codes

Another debate which reveals the extent to which multiculturalism is taken seriously, revolves around dress codes and grooming policies. In a number of conflicts the issue has been whether or not ethnic minorities could be exempt from a dress code policy. Canadian institutions have sometimes been willing to allow Sikhs to wear religious symbols like turbans and kirpans. For example, in 1990 despite litigation challenging the policy,[45] the Royal Canadian Mounted Police (RCMP) continued to allow baptized Sikhs to wear their turbans instead of the traditional Mountie Stetson as this posed no real threat to Canadian's core values.[46] The reaction was quite hostile, and the case was taken on appeal.[47]

In another case, *K.S. Bhinder and the Canadian Human Rights Commission v. Canadian National Railway Company* (1985),[48] the question was whether wearing a hard hat was a bona fide occupational requirement. The railway decided to institute a rule that all employees wear a safety helmet at a particular work site. Bhinder, a Sikh employee, refused to comply with the rule because a turban was the only type of head-gear permitted by his religion. The company refused to make an exception, and Bhinder rejected other work not requiring a hard hat.

The Canadian Human Tribunal, upon finding that Canadian National Railway Co. had discriminated by imposing the rule, ordered Bhinder's reinstatement and compensation for loss of salary. The Federal Court of Appeal set that decision aside on the ground that the new regulation was not, in fact, discriminatory. The Supreme Court of Canada held that the appeal should be dismissed because the hard hat rule was a bona fide occupational requirement. Even if a working condition results in a discriminatory practice, this does not per se invalidate its status as a bona fide occupational requirement. The Court found no violation of the Canadian Human Rights Act since there was no duty to accommodate where a valid bona fide occupational requirement existed.

The majority of the Supreme Court disagreed with the Court of Appeal that the Human Rights Act applied only to intentional discrimination and stated that it extends to unintentional and adverse effect discrimination.[49] None of the judges appear to have considered the possibility that a special helmet might be constructed which Sikhs might be persuaded to wear over their turbans.[50]

In *Hothi et al. v. Regina*[51], the judge refused to allow a Sikh defendant to wear his kirpan, a ceremonial dagger, in the courtroom. The judge may have had cause for alarm since this particular defendant was charged with assault! However, the defendant presumably did not use his kirpan (assuming he was guilty), as it is as preposterous to suggest to a Sikh person that a kirpan, a religious symbol, would be used as a weapon as it would be to suggest to a Christian that a crucifix would be used in that way.

15

In the United States there is also a lack of willingness to allow ethnic minorities to wear symbols central to their identity. Sometimes the denial of the right is justified on the grounds of a public safety threat,[52] sometimes because of a conflict with the corporate image,[53] and sometimes based on aesthetics. The courts in Canada and the United States have both been disinclined to promote multiculturalism in the context of dress and grooming policies in many instances.

Language Policy

Another key indicator of difference among groups is language. In the Canadian context the language policy has been complicated. There are three major parts of Canadian language policy: "bilingualism in federal institutions, preservation and promotion of French outside Quebec, preservation and promotion of English in Quebec."[54] There is an assumption that Canada is successful with multiculturalism because of the adoption of bilingual policies. However, this policy was adopted under duress. The historical record shows ongoing pressure to make English the only official language. Allowing French to be spoken was necessary to avoid Canada's being absorbed by the United States; afterwards there was pressure to shift to an "English only" policy.[55]

The bilingual policy was weak at the outset. The 1867 British North America Act has a limited guarantee of bilingualism which is found in Section 133:

> Either the English or the French Language may be used by any Person in the Debates of the Houses of the Parliament of Canada and of the Houses of the Legislature of Quebec; and both those Languages shall be used in the respective Records and Journals of the Houses; and either of those languages may be used by any Person or in any Pleading or Process in or issuing from any Court of Canada established under this Act and in or from all or any of the Court of Quebec.
> The Acts of the Parliament of Canada and of the Legislature of

Quebec shall be printed and published in both those Languages.

Nevertheless, the policy has not been championed vigorously and has not been followed consistently. Apparently it was more useful in protecting the English language in Quebec than in protecting the use of French in the rest of Canada.[56] Courts have not permitted Quebec's attempt to mitigate the effect of Section 133.

Other laws have been adopted to protect bilingualism including the 1969 Official Languages Act, which mandates equal status for the two languages in federal institutions, and by the constitutional guarantees in the 1982 Charter guaranteeing total bilingualism. Until the 1960s, federal government institutions did not use French. The Official Languages Act was enacted in 1969 but it did not make Canada totally bilingual as it only applied to matters with the federal powers; it did not have constitutional character.[57] It expanded the use of French across Canada[58] where at least ten percent of the population spoke a minority language. The response to the implementation of the law was "a distressing English backlash against bilingualism."[59]

Bilingualism has not been a success altogether in Quebec either. Quebec nationalists often boast that the Anglophone community is the world's best treated minority.[60] Bilingualism is said to be most successful because the English speaking minority has access to many services like hospitals, schools, and universities which are unavailable to Francophone minorities outside of Quebec. Ironically, however, there have been efforts to narrow the scope of rights for linguistic minorities. For instance, a controversy raged over having commercial signs in French only, but the courts invalidated this policy. The courts have held that bilingual signs pose no threat to French and laws may not prohibit the use of English.[61] Another policy which demonstrates the degree to which English is only tolerated is Quebec cinema law. Quebec tried to enforce a right to show English films contingent upon the availability of a French version with certain exceptions.[62] Since the 1970s the governments in Quebec also tried to assimilate immigrants to French culture (rather than the English one).[63-64]

The mass exodus of English speakers from Quebec[65] may suggest that something is amiss with the successful bilingual policy. Furthermore, the political movement in Quebec to secede indicates that it is not content with a bilingual policy in a multicultural context.

Questions remain concerning the meaning of the bilingual policy in Canada. If during a trial a defendant chooses English, does this require that the prosecutor speak English or is it acceptable for the prosecutor to speak French provided the defendant has an interpreter? Courts have reached opposite conclusions. Another issue is how to handle discrepancies in the English and French versions. It appears that the interpretation should be that which best gives effect to the legislators' intent.

Even though there is a widespread perception that Canada protects cultural rights, including language rights, Canada's language policies afford protection only to one language other than English, namely French. For the most part, the other languages known as 'heritage languages' have not been the subject of concern.

In order to determine whether language rights are protected more generally in Canada, it would be useful to know, as an empirical matter, the extent to which language preservation efforts have succeeded. In 1975 the government authorized funds for heritage language programs, an acknowledgment that language and ethnicity are inextricably linked. In 1984, due in part to pressure, the government decided to promote heritage languages for the benefit of the ethnic minorities as well as for the benefit of all Canadians.

One empirical study of language use in Canada examined whether the support for heritage languages resulted in their being spoken more at home. It found: "the heritage language protection has made no measurable positive national impact on the retention of heritage languages as reported by the respondents concerning the census question language of the home."[66] Despite attempts at language preservation, Canadians appear to be losing their ability to converse in other languages. If other languages are lost, then this has profound implications for the multiculturalism vision in Canada. They express their worry: "If language is synonymous with ethnicity, the linguistic trends possibly profoundly undermine the multicultural vision."[67]

Canada is often cited as a linguistic pluralism success story. As discussed, it is important to bear in mind that the pluralistic policy was adopted under duress, it was a bilingual rather than a multilingual policy, and that there have been concerted efforts to narrow the scope of rights for linguistic minorities.

The Impact of Multiculturalism in Canada

What has multiculturalism accomplished in Canada? The evidence is not entirely clear as to the positive effects of multiculturalism there. The policy has not prevented racism nor has it helped English Canadians to establish a national identity.[68]

The policy has been criticized on several grounds. First, some assert that the effort to promote individual identities has undermined Canadian national unity. Second, some minorities regard the policy as "mere rhetoric, a tool for buying the ethnic vote, and a means of perpetuating the power of English Canadian elites."[69] Third, some view it as a policy designed to thwart Quebec's efforts to secede. Others consider the policy anachronistic because it was originally designed with European immigrants in mind; the government was principally concerned with cultural promotion and language retention. Newer immigrants favor a more ambitious multiculturalism. In fact, the current mandate of the Department of Multiculturalism and Citizenship is to combat racism and racial discrimination. Evidently, multiculturalism is being interpreted more broadly in the 1990s.[70]

In reality, multiculturalism is not necessarily divisive. Immigrants in Canada, after an initial period of adjustment, seem to participate in Canadian public life. Despite their successful cultural adaptation, there is a perception that they cause trouble. High profile cases, such as Sikh challenges to dress codes may create this impression.[71]

A Comparative Perspective

The crux of the issue is the extent to which law protects the rights to culture. In the final analysis, Canada's official policy of multiculturalism is superior to the U.S. policy, or non-policy. In the U.S. there is no explicit guarantee of this type of right, no recognition of culture, one way or the other. Since there is a constitutional right to the free exercise of religion, cultural arguments that can be forced to fit the category of religion may be given legal force. There remains, however, the problem of the belief/action distinction according to which beliefs are absolutely protected but religiously motivated actions usually are not.[72] Specific policies pertaining to the protection of sacred sites[73] reflect a concern with culture, but the abstract right itself is not explicitly protected in American law.

In the implementation process, oddly enough, the U.S. sometimes has shown greater cultural sensitivity in the context of particular legal disputes. Both countries could facilitate greater accommodation of cultural differences by following the model of cultural pluralism. If they continue to adhere to the model of forced assimilation, their policies will deny many their constitutional rights, and ultimately alienate cultural minorities completely from the system.

Having ratified the International Covenant on Civil and Political Rights, Canada and the U.S. are obligated to guarantee the right to culture in Article 27. The Human Rights Committee, which is empowered to monitor compliance with treaty obligations, has issued General Comment 23 giving its interpretation to this article. According to the interpretation of Article 27 in the comment States Parties must take affirmative steps to effectuate the rights enumerated in Article 27. Though the Article has been criticized, for instance, for relying on individualistic conceptions of rights rather than group rights when the latter may be more appropriate for language, culture, and religion, it is the best vehicle for protecting multiculturalism at the present time. States will find Article 27 to be a useful tool for defending the policy of multiculturalism.

Conclusion

In this essay I have provided a brief overview of Canada's policy of multiculturalism. Changes in immigration patterns have occurred, resulting in most immigrants coming from Asia, Africa, Latin America, and the Caribbean rather than from Europe, as had previously been the case. This phenomenon has contributed to greater anxiety about Canadian national identity, because it is widely believed that the new immigrants will not be able to become assimilated, i.e., "Canadianized."[74] Consequently there is in Canada, as in the United States, an anti-immigrant, anti-multiculturalism mood. In Canada, the result appears to be a backlash again the policy of multiculturalism.[75]

Despite the negative reactions to the policy, there has been a much more concerted effort to institutionalize recognition of cultural differences in Canada than in other countries, including the United States. Although the implementation of the policy may leave something to be desired, as the case studies showed, at least there is a commitment to the basic principles at stake. With the establishment of new legal instruments like Article 27 of the International Covenant on Civil and Political Rights, multiculturalism may eventually have the force of law.

NOTES

1. Sarah Wayland (1997). Immigration, Multiculturalism, and National Identity in Canada. *International Journal on Minority and Group Rights 5*, p. 33.
2. Leslie S. Laczko (1994). Canada's Pluralism in Comparative Perspective. *Ethnic and Racial Studies* 17, 20-41.
3. John Herd Thompson and Morton Weinfeld (1995). Entry and Exit: Canadian Immigration Policy in Context. *The Annals of the American Academy of Political and Social Science* 538, p. 197.
4. For analysis of these two models, see the classic by Milton M. Gordon (1964). *Assimilation in American Life: The Role of Race, Religion, and National Origins.* New York: Oxford University Press.
5. Will Kymlicka (1995). *Multicultural Citizenship: A Liberal Theory of Minority Rights.* Oxford: Clarendon Press. See also his edited collection (1995) *The Rights of Minority Cultures* (New York: Oxford University Press. For a critique, see Brian Walker (1997). Plural Cultures, Contested Territories: A Critique of Kymlicka. *Canadian Journal of Political Science* 30, pp. 211-234.
6. Laczko argues this contrast is a "misleading" oversimplification of the Canadian experience (p. 23). Despite this observation, however, Laczko concludes that Canada is more pluralistic than other nations (p. 38).
7. Wayland, supra note 1, analyzes the "backlash" thesis and reviews relevant studies on the question.
8. See Reginald W. Bibby (1990). *Mosaic Madness: Poverty and Potential of life in Canada.* Toronto: Stoddart. See also Neil Bissoondath (1993). A question of Belonging: Multiculturalism and Citizenship. In William Kaplan (Ed.) *Belonging: The Meaning and Future of Canadian Citizenship* (pp.368-387). Montreal & Kingston: McGill-Queen's University Press.
9. Patricia Roy (1995). The Fifth Force : Multiculturalism and the English Canadian Identity. *The Annals of the American Academy of Political and Social Science* 538, p. 201.
10. For a survey of critiques, see Yasmeen Abu-Laban and Daiva Stasiulis (1992). Ethnic Pluralism under Siege: Popular and Partisan Opposition to Multiculturalism. *Canadian Public Policy* 18, pp. 365-386.
11. See, e.g., Thompson and Weinfeld, supra note 3, p. 194.
12. Darlene Johnston (1993). First Nations and Canadian Citizenship. In William Kaplan (Ed.) *Belonging: The Meaning and Future of Canadian Citizenship* (pp. 349-

367). Montreal & Kingston: McGill-Queen's University Press.

13. Ibid., p. 363.

14. Thompson and Weinfeld, supra note 3, p. 186.

15. Goldwin Smith (1971). *Canada and the Canadian Question.* Toronto: University of Toronto Press, p. 233. Quoted in Thompson and Weinfeld, supra note 2, p. 186.

16. "...[they] had not the slightest notion of encouraging a multicultural mosaic in which immigrants would retain the languages and cultures they brought with them to Canada." Thompson and Weinfeld, supra note 3, p. 188.

17. Julius Grey (1993). Language and Canadian Public Law. In William Kaplan and Donald McRae (Eds.) *Law, Policy, and International Justice: Essays in Honour of Maxwell Cohen.* Montreal & Kingston: McGill-Queen's University Press, p. 321.

18. Grey refers to this as "one of the most shameful episodes in Canadian history", p. 331.

19. See, e.g., Thompson and Weinfeld, supra note 3, p. 187.

20. Wayland, supra note 1, p. 37.

21. Ibid., pp. 39-40.

22. This categorization comes from Thompson and Weinfeld, supra note 3, p. 188.

23. This information comes from Thompson and Weinfeld, supra note 3, p. 189.

24. Wayland, supra note 1, p. 50.

25. Ibid.

26. Interestingly, Trudeau noted that First Nations peoples had to make a tough decision: "...the time is now to decide whether the Indians will be a race apart in Canada or whether [they] will be Canadians of full status. And this is a difficult choice. It must be a very agonizing choice to Indian peoples themselves because, on the one hand, they realize that if they come into society as total citizens they will be equal under the law but they risk losing certain of their traditions, certain aspects of a culture and perhaps even certain of their basic rights." Quoted in Johnston, p. 364.

27. Canadian Prime Minister Pierre Trudeau publicly stated: "The government will support and encourage the various cultures and ethnic groups that give structure and vitality to our society. They will be encouraged to share their cultural expression and values with other Canadians and so contribute to a richer life for us all" Quoted in Wayland, supra note 1, p. 33.

28. Clement Hobbs, Ian Lee, and George Haines (1991). Implementing Multicultural Policy: an Analysis of the Heritage Language Program, 1971-1981. *Canadian Public Administration* 34, pp. 664-675.

29. Ibid., p. 666.

30. For an interesting analysis of the distinction between integration and assimilation, see John C. Harles (1997). Integration before Assimilation: Immigration, Multiculturalism and the Canadian Polity. *Canadian Journal of Political Science* 333, pp. 711-736.

31. Canada, House of Commons, *Debates*, 3rd session, vol.115 (October 8, 1971), p. 8546. Quoted in Hobbs et al, pp. 666-667.

32. For an evaluation of the Charter's influence generally, see Philip Bryden, Steven Davis, and John Russell (Eds.) (1994) *Protecting Rights and Freedoms: Essays on the Charter's Place in Canada's Political, Legal, and Intellectual Life.* Toronto: University

23

of Toronto Press. See also Evelyn Kallen (1995). *Ethnicity and Human Rights in Canada* (2nd edition). Toronto: Oxford University Press., Chapter 10 "The Legal Framework for Protection of Minority Rights in Canada: The Canadian Constitution and its Charter of Rights and Freedoms."

33. The Department of Justice circulated a consultation paper Reforming the General Part of the Criminal Code which include section II. Defences h) Culture as a defense, pp. 23-24.

34. Anon. (1994, November 17). Should culture be a criminal defence? *The Globe and Mail.* Daryl-Lynn Carlson (1994, November. 21-27). Ottawa study revamping part of Criminal Code: Culture, intoxication as possible defenses. *Law Times,* p. 7. Douglas Fisher (1994, November 16). A Rock Solid Performance. *The Toronto Sun*, p. 11.

35. R. v. Ly (1987). 33 C.C.C. (3d) 31, p. 33.

36. R. v. Ly (1987), p. 38.

37. Macfarlane presented the judgement, giving a careful reading to the Supreme Court decision of *R. v. Hill* (1986). 1 R.C.S. 313.

It established that while jurors may ascribe characteristics to the ordinary person for the purposes of a given case, the judge is not required to tell the jury what specific attributes it should ascribe. In *Hill* the Court said:

For example, if the provocation is a racial slur, the jury will think of an ordinary person with the racial background that forms the substance of the insult. To this extent, particular characteristics will be ascribed to the ordinary person. Indeed it would be impossible to conceptualize a sexless or ageless ordinary person (p.36)

Surprisingly, Macfarlane rejected the appellant's argument that culture was pertinent to the ordinary person test. He says that the Vietnamese cultural background "might have been relevant to the first question if a racial slur had been involved, but that is not the case" (p.38). To justify this conclusion and discuss the appeal, he refers to the Hill decision which, despite the earlier language accepting the attribution of traits, portrays the ordinary person standard as one "expected of all in society".

38. *People v. Aphaylath* (1986a). 499 N.Y.S. 2d. 823 (A.D. 4 Dept.); *People v. Aphaylath* (1986b). 502 N.E.2d 998 (N.Y.).

39. *Jack and Charlie v. R.* 1985 at 91. *Jack and Charlie v. R.* (1985). 4 Canadian Native Law Reporter, 88-102. [Supreme Court of Canada]. (1982). 139 Dominion Law Reports (3rd series; 1983), 25-44. [British Columbia Court of Appeal]. (1979). 50 Canadian Criminal Cases (2nd series; 1980), 337-365. [British Columbia Provincial Court].

40. Louise Mandell (1987). Native Culture on Trial. In Sheilah L. Martin and Kathleen E. Mahony (Eds.) *Equality and Judicial Neutrality* (pp. 358-365). Toronto: Carswell, p. 362.

41. *Jack and Charlie v. R.* 1985 at 88.

The Court stated: "There was no evidence that the use of defrosted raw deer meat was sacrilegious as is alleged in appellants' factum, there was no evidence that the killing of the deer was part of the religious ceremony" (1985 at 100) But the defense counsel, Mandell noted: "It is significant that although the judges could envision a proper burning with stored deer meat, the Indians could not" (1987 at 363). Her essay discusses the case as an example of judicial bias, focusing on the Court's failure to understand the Indian worldview.

43. *Jack and Charlie v. R.* 1985, p. 102. In criminal law, the only elements needed for a conviction are *mens rea* or intent and *actus reus* or the act; motive is irrelevant for the determination of guilt or innocence, though it may be considered during sentencing for purposes of mitigation.

44. *State v. Berry,* 707 P.2d 638 (Or App. 1985).

45. *In Lethbridge RCMP Veterans Court Challenge Committee v. Attorney General of Canada* (Attorney General) the plaintiffs sought an order to prevent the RCMP from allowing religious symbols as part of the official uniform. Federal Court of Appeals, 31 CRR 2d 370 (May 31, 1995). 1994 F.C.J. No. 1001. 94 *Canadian Labour Law Reports* 12, 204.

46. Roy, supra note, p. 207; Thompson and Weinfeld, supra note, pp. 195-196. In 1995 the Federal Court of Appeal upheld the RCMP uniform policy of allowing religious accommodation.

47. In 1995 the Federal Court of Appeal upheld the RCMP uniform policy of allowing religious accommodation.

48. *K.S. Bhinder and the Canadian Human Rights Commission v. Canadian National Railway Company,* [1985] S.C.R. Canada Supreme Court Reports; also published in *Canadian Human Rights Reporter* Vol.7, Decision 488 (January 1986).

49. For further explanation of this doctrine, see Milton Woodward (1987). A Qualification on the Duty of Employers to Accommodate Religious Practices: K.S. Bhinder and the Canadian Human Rights Commission v. the Canadian National Railway Company. *University of British Columbia Law Review* 21, pp. 471-494. See also Ivan F. Ivankovich (1986-1987). The Religious Employee and Reasonable Accommodation Requirements. *Canadian Business Law Journal* 13, pp. 313-358.

50. The Human Rights Committee to which Bhinder submitted a communication alleging violation of his right to religious freedom under Article 18 of the International Covenant of Civil and Political Rights, also concluded that Bhinder's rights had not been violated. *Bhinder v. Canada,* Communication No.208/1986. International Law Reports 96, pp. 660-666.

51. *Hothi et al. v. Regina* 1985. 3 Western Weekly Reports 256. The defendant challenged the ruling of the Provincial Judge excluding his kirpan from the courtroom. The judge's ruling was affirmed by the Manitoba Court of Appeal 35 Manitoba reports 2d 159 (1985) and the Supreme Court of Canada denied review.

52. This was the rationale in *Cheema v. Thompson* in which Sikh children wearing the kirpan were not allowed to attend school due to the "no weapons" policy. *Cheema v. Thompson,* 67 F.3d 883 (April 18, 1995), 1994 U.S. App. LEXIS 24160 (unpublished decision, September 2, 1994).

Eventually the Ninth Circuit ruled that the children had to be permitted to go to school, provided the kirpans were blunt or glued into the sheath. Safety was also central to *Bhatia v. Chevron,* 734 F.2d 1382 (1984), in which a Sikh employee unable to wear a gas mask because of the beard he was required to wear.

53. *In LOOC, INC. d/b/a/ Domino's Pizza v. Prabhjot S. Kohli,* 347 Md. 258, 701 A.2d

92 (October 9, 1997), the issue was whether Domino's Pizza refusal to hire Mr. Kohli as a manager unless he shaved off his beard because if its company-wide no beard policy violated Maryland civil rights law. After ten years of litigation, the Maryland Court of Appeals concluded that the original tribunal lacked the authority to force Domino's to change its policy. Andrea F. Siegel (1997, October 10). After 10 Years, Court Rules on No-Beard Policy. *The Baltimore Sun,* p.3B.

54. Grey, supra note, p. 322.

55. It is also noteworthy that the French were Catholic and the English Protestants. The religious difference compounded the problems associated with the cleavage over language. Dale Thompson (1995). Language, Identity and the Nationalist Impulse: Quebec. *The Annals of the American Academy of Political and Social Science* 583, p. 74.

56. Grey, supra note, p. 323.

57. Grey, supra note, p. 327.

58. The policy applied to "bilingual districts" where at least 10 percent of the population spoke with minority language. Grey, p. 327.

59. Grey, supra note, p. 328.

60. Grey, supra note, p. 335.

61. For further discussion of this debate, see Thompson 1995, pp. 76-77.

62. At least films subtitled in French count as a French version. See Grey, p. 348.

63. Thompson discusses this Quebec policy, p. 79. When Thompson and Weinfeld say that the "French Canadians were even more 'reluctant hosts' to immigrants than were English Canadians," they mean presumably they were even more eager to promote assimilation. Thompson and Weinfeld, supra note 3, p. 188.

64. It also tried to ensure that current members identified with French culture. One example was Quebec's effort to improve the status of French by "bringing it into line with the international variety of French" in order to promote Francophone community identity. Thompson, p. 75.

65. Grey, p. 337.

66. Hobbs, Lee, and Haines, p. 672.

67. Hobbs, Lee, and Haines, p. 673.

68. Roy, p. 199.

69. Wayland, p. 48.

70. Wayland, p. 49.

71. Thompson and Weinfeld, p. 195.

72. The Religious Freedom Restoration Act (42 U.S.C. 2000bb (1994)) seems to afford greater protection, but its validity is currently being litigated.

73. For instance, President Clinton issued Executive Order 13007 Indian Sacred Sites on May 24, 1996. 32 Weekly Comp. Pres. Doc. 942.

74. One scholar questions whether immigrants can be assimilated: "The ambiguity of Canadianness suggests that conceptually there is little for immigrants to assimilate into, and no certain focus for their political identity... Should a country lack a clear understanding of its national character, it would seem also to lack the ability to equip immigrants with the collective convictions that mark a cohesive political community". See

Harle, pp. 713-714.

75. One result of the anti-immigrant, anti-multiculturalism trend is that the Canadian government moved immigration to a new Super Ministry of Public Security.

References

Abu-Laban, Yasmeen and Daiva Stasiulis (1992). Ethnic Pluralism under Siege: Popular and Partisan Opposition to Multiculturalism. *Canadian Public Policy* 18, pp. 365-386.

Anon. (1994, November 17). Should culture be a criminal defense? The *Globe and Mail.*

Bhatia v. Chevron, 734 F.2d 1382 (1984)

K.S. Bhinder and the Canadian Human Rights Commission v. Canadian National Railway Company, [1985] S.C.R. (*Canada Supreme Court Reports; also published in Canadian Human Rights Reporter* Vol. 7, Decision 488 (January 1986).

Bhinder v. Canada, Communication No. 208/1986. *International Law Reports* 96, pp. 660-666.

Bibby, Reginald W. (1990). *Mosaic Madness: Poverty and Potential of Life in Canada.* Toronto: Stoddart.

Bissoondath, Neil (1993). A Question of Belonging: Multiculturalism and Citizenship. In William Kaplan (Ed.) *Belonging: The Meaning and Future of Canadian Citizenship* (pp. 368-387). Montreal & Kingston: McGill-Queen's University Press.

Bryden, Philip, Steven Davis, and John Russell (Eds.) (1994) *Protecting Rights and Freedoms: Essays on the Charter's Place in Canada's Political, Legal, and Intellectual Life.* Toronto: University of Toronto Press.

Carlson, Daryl-Lynn (1994, November. 21-27). Ottawa study revamping part of Criminal Code: Culture, intoxication as possible defenses. *Law Times.*
Cheema v. Thompson, 67 F.3d 883 (April 18, 1995),1994 U.S. App. LEXIS 24160 (unpublished decision, September 2, 1994).

Clinton, William President. Executive Order 13007 ñ Indian Sacred Sites on May 24, 1996. 32 *Weekly Comp. Pres.* Doc. 942.

Fisher, Douglas (1994, November 16). A Rock Solid Performance. *The Toronto Sun,* p.11.

Gordon, Milton M. (1964). *Assimilation in American Life. The Role of Race, Religion, and National Origins.* New York: Oxford University Press.

Grey, Julius (1993). Language and Canadian Public Law. In William Kaplan and

Donald McRae (Eds.) *Law, Policy, and International Justice: Essays in Honour of Maxwell Cohen* (pp. 320-362). Montreal & Kingston: McGill-Queen's University Press.

Harles, John C. (1997). Integration before Assimilation: Immigration, Multiculturalism and the Canadian Polity. *Canadian Journal of Political Science* 333, pp.711-736.

Hobbs, Clement, Ian Lee, and George Haines (1991). Implementing Multicultural Policy: an Analysis of the Heritage Language Program, 1971-1981. *Canadian Public Administration* 34, pp. 664-675.

Hothi et al. v. Regina (1985) 3 Western Weekly Reports 256. 35 Manitoba Reports 2d 159 (1985).

Human Rights Committee (1994). *General Comment No.23 on Article 27 of the Covenant.* CCPR/C/21/Rev.1/Add.4, 25 April, 1994.

Ivankovich, Ivan F. (1986-1987). The Religious Employee and Reasonable Accommodation Requirements. *Canadian Business Law Journal* 13, pp. 313-358.

Jack and Charlie v. R. 1985 at 91. *Jack and Charlie v. R.* (1985). 4 Canadian Native Law Reporter, 88-102. [Supreme Court of Canada]. (1982). 139 Dominion Law Reports (3rd series; 1983), 25-44. [British Columbia Court of Appeal].(1979). 50 Canadian Criminal Cases (2nd series; 1980), 337-345. [British Columbia Provincial Court].

Johnston, Darlene (1993). First Nations and Canadian Citizenship. In William Kaplan (Ed.) *Belonging: The Meaning and Future of Canadian Citizenship* (pp. 349-367). Montreal & Kingston: McGill-Queenís University Press.

Kallen, Evelyn (1995). *Ethnicity and Human Rights in Canada* (2nd edition). Toronto: Oxford University Press., Chapter 10 iThe Legal Framework for Protection of Minority Rights in Canada: The Canadian Constitution and its Charter of Rights and Freedoms.

Kymlicka, Will (1995). *Multicultural Citizenship: A Liberal Theory of Minority Rights.* Oxford: Clarendon Press.

Kymlicka, Will (Ed.) (1995) *The Rights of Minority Cultures* (New York: Oxford University Press).

Laczko, Leslie S. (1994). Canada's Pluralism in Comparative Perspective. *Ethnic and Racial Studies* 17, 20-41.

Lethbridge RCMP *Veterans' Court Challenge Committee v. Attorney General of Canada.* 1994 F.C.J. No.1001. 94 Canadian Labour Law Reports 12, 204.

LOOC INC. d/b/a/ *Domino's Pizza v. Prabhjot S. Kohli,* 347 Md. 258, 701, A.2d 92 (October 9, 1997).

Mandell, Louise (1987). Native Culture on Trial. In Sheilah L. Martin and Kathleen E. Mahoney (Eds.) *Equality and Judicial Neutrality* (pp. 358-365). Toronto: Carswell, p.

362.

Pal, Leslie A. (1993). *Interests of State: The Politics of Language, Multiculturalism, and Feminism in Canada.* Montreal & Kingston: McGill-Queen's University Press.

People v. Aphaylath (1986a). 499 N.Y.S. 2d. 823 (A.D. 4 Dept.); *People v. Aphaylath* (1986b). 502 N.E.2d 998 (N.Y.).

Peter, Karl (1981). The Myth of Multiculturalism and Other Political Fables. In Jorgen Dahlie and Tissa Fernando (Eds.) *Ethnicity, Power, and Politics in Canada* (pp. 56-67). Toronto: Methuen.

R. v. Hill (1986). 1 R.C.S. 313.

R. v. Ly (1987). 33 C.C.C. (3d) 31, p. 33.

Roy, Patricia (1995). The Fifth Force: Multiculturalism and the English Canadian Identity. *The Annals of the American Academy of Political and Social Science* 538, pp. 199-209.

Siegal, Andrea F. (1997, October 10). After 10 Years, Court Rules on No-Beard Policy. *The Baltimore Sun,* p.3B.

Smith, Goldwin (1971). *Canada and the Canadian Question.* Toronto: University of Toronto Press.

State v. Berry (1985). 707 P.2d 638.

Thompson, John Herd and Morton Weinfeld (1995). Entry and Exit: Canadian Immigration Policy in Context. *The Annals of the American Academy of Political and Social Science* 538, pp. 185-198.

Thomson, Dale (1995). Language, Identity, and the Nationalist Impulse: Quebec. *The Annals of the American Academy of Political and Social Science* 538, pp. 69-82.

Walker, Brian (1997). Plural Cultures, Contested Territories: A Critique of Kymlicka. *Canadian Journal of Political Science* 30, pp. 211-234.

Wayland, Sarah (1997). Immigration, Multiculturalism, and National Identity in Canada. *International Journal on Minority and Group Rights* 5, pp. 33-58.

Woodard, Milton(1987). A Qualification on the Duty of Employers to Accommodate Religious Practices: *K.S. Bhinder and the Canadian Human Rights Commission v. the Canadian National Railway Company. University of British Columbia Law Review* 21, pp. 471-494.

CHAPTER II

MULTICULTURALISM IN MEXICO: THE ZAPATISTA CHALLENGE
Gloria Yolanda Guevara *

In a world where ethnic struggles have supplanted the Cold War as the major threat to peace, both developed and underdeveloped societies face the challenges of multiethnicity within their borders.
Laura Carlson, *Journalist*

Culture and cultural identities are shaping the patterns of cohesion, disintegration, and conflict in the post-Cold War world.
Samuel Huntington, *Clash of Civilizations*

We fight to gain respect for our dignity. What offends us most is the inability to express our sentiments, our demands. Let it be clear that we fight for our dignity as Indians and so that we will not be stigmatized. For years we have not been respected...We say this in order that we stop being treated like animals in a zoo, so that we get treated as persons, humans and Indians.
Juan, *Delegate to the 1994 Peace Accords in Chiapas*

Scholars such as Samuel Huntington argue that the greatest threat to peace will emerge from the clash of cultures or civilizations, that *ethnic struggles have supplanted the Cold War as the major threat to peace.* Huntington contends that Latin American countries pose a relatively small threat to world peace and economic stability especially since the end of the Cold War. However, the event that transpired on January 1, 1994 challenges Huntington's assumption. Mexico reflects vast cultural, geographic, ideological, political and socioeconomic diversity. The Chiapas uprising conveys how a small group of Indians can indeed pose a threat to the global arena, in attempting to derail a major international trade agreement such as NAFTA.[1]

---

* **Gloria Yolanda Guevara is a Doctoral Candidate in Political Science, University of Southern California.**

The guerrilla uprising in the small southern state of Chiapas introduced the world to the Zapatistas -- a group of armed Indians that had a simple message to the Mexican government and the world: *Hoy Decimos Basta!* (Today we say enough!). This rebellion underscores the tensions felt by the indigenous populations over the years that included repressive policies and discriminatory practices which continue to play an integral part in defining Mexico's history. The December 27, 1997 massacre of 45 men, women and children in the small community of Acteal, in the highlands of Chiapas, by the Mexican government further illustrates the idea that historically, the Indians have been viewed as a "problem". Underlying the continued violence in Chiapas is a native Indian culture that has traditionally been viewed as an embarrassment to many Mexicans and to the government. For many Mexicans, such backwardness is seen as a barrier to modernization.

The Zapatista rebellion also called attention to the destabilizing effects, specifically the negative socioeconomic impact of economic restructuring. The socioeconomic changes have had a negative effect in that they tend to reinforce the cultural cleavages between the Indians and the rest of Mexican society. Such cleavages, reinforced by vast differentiation in economic status between the indigenous groups and much of Mexican society, have been a characteristic of Mexican history since its early colonization.

The violence in Chiapas highlights the complexities that surround the question of peaceful coexistence among the Mexican people which consist of different ethnic groups (even among the ingenious populations). Moreover, it reiterates the notion that the Mexican state has little respect for the indigenous peoples and their right to cultural autonomy.

Who are the Zapatistas? How does the revolt reflect larger global processes? The purpose of this essay is to address the factors surrounding the Zapatista rebellion through a historical account of the changing state-society relations between the Mexican state and the indigenous groups, incorporating the impact of the legacy of colonization and the Revolution of 1910. After the Revolution, the state sought to create a national identity, which carried implications for different groups within Mexico. Such groups based their identities on specific (and differing) interpretations of the Revolution. This paper posits that recent attempts by the Mexican government to abandon much of the discourse of the Revolution is a clear attempt to redefine it, therefore directly challenging the types of identities formed by the Revolution. This assumption holds true for the Indians of Chiapas.

The first part of the analysis explores the development of the identities that were shaped as a result of Spanish colonization and the Revolution. The second part examines the Salinas administration (1988-1994), its new economic model, and the changes associated with this shift in development strategy which have had a direct impact on indigenous groups in Mexico. A historical account of the changing socioeconomic relations between the state and society serves as an explanatory variable in unveiling the factors surrounding the Chiapas uprising. The violence in the region underscores the idea that, historically, indigenous groups in Mexico do not enjoy the same status or human rights as other Mexican citizens.

Constructing Identity in Mexico: The Legacy of Colonialism & Revolution

The ideology and legacy of the Revolution of 1910 is not necessarily the first historical event to present a picture of Mexican society, or of a national identity.[2] Colonial Mexican society also left behind the legacy of a social hierarchy. This social hierarchy did not simply reflect a stratum with whites on top, mestizos in the middle and Indians and blacks on the bottom.[3] Rather, Aitken (1996) argues, it reflects a triangle with "a variety of different castes existing between the three poles of pure blood." He also argues that "the emergence of this system therefore linked race and culture. Spanish domination was legitimated by its greater purity, expressed not only in religion but also in purity of blood."[4] *Gente de razon* (civilized people or whites) were contrasted with *naturales* (Indians). In colonial Mexico, social status was based not only on economic position but also on culture, and this legacy still exists in present-day Mexican society. Urban social groups in Mexico continue to define their identities partially in terms of the *gente de razon*, and set themselves apart from the poor Indians in terms of education and culture. This is apparent in the discourse that continues to blame Mexico's incomplete democracy on the backwardness and lack of sophistication associated with *naturales*. Such characteristics, according to more sophisticated urban dwellers, do not serve the promotion of proper democratic culture.[5] Thus in Mexico, class became configured with race and the term Indian became synonymous with poverty and cultural backwardness. However, the rich could be "whitened."[6]

With the revolution, the ideology has been central in the construction of local identities for social groups while reinforcing the identities that were a result of the legacy of the colonial period. Interestingly, Knight (1990) demonstrates that the regional identity that was shaped by both colonization and revolution has remained greater than the imagined "national" identity falsely constructed by the Mexican state. Supporting this finding, Aitken (1996) argues that in the region of Michoacan the emphasis on individual identity and private property is characteristic of the ranchero communities that emphasize honor, dignity, manliness, courage and individual skills. These communities identify themselves as "white" stressing their European heritage, and refuse any social ties with indigenous communities, even those located within the region.[7] Such ranchero communities also have a negative view of Indians and mestizo ejiditarios, who are dismissed as clients of the state and are viewed as being dependent upon the state for their identity and survival.

But while in the northern region of Mexico the identity formed as a result of colonization and revolution was that of individual rights (liberalism), in the southern regions populated by indigenous groups, identities reflected that of communal or group identities. For these groups, the ideology of the Mexican Revolution reflected different notions than those found in Michoacan, such as communalism, participation, economic redistribution, and social justice. Although government actions were often at odds with the substantive and procedural content of revolutionary ideals, in different regions the ideas associated with the 1910-20 Revolution had enduring importance for Mexican politics and the identities formed in this context. It also influenced the interpretation of what the "social contract" between the different groups within Mexico and the Mexican state represented.[8]

The Post - Revolutionary Mexican State

The particular vision of this imagined community in post-revolutionary Mexico was one in which the State sat above society and acted, at least in the official discourse, as an arbitrator between different social groups. The totaling vision of the modern nation-state has the effect of politicizing social and cultural issues, which now must be resolved in the public domain with reference to the State. Struggles over land become struggles of State recognition of land claims. At the same time, official discourses and new bureaucratic structures of representation such as trade unions, peasant unions, ejidos (land reform communities) have the effect of categorizing people as workers, peasants or ejidatarios.[9]

In post-revolutionary Mexico, Cardenas was the first president who took steps to carry out the principles of the Revolution.[10] Cardenas sought to attain national sovereignty by gaining control over certain key sectors of the society (i.e., peasants and workers), and destroying others (the power of the traditional land owning sector, the Church) and encouraging the growth of private capital while controlling the influences of foreign capital. Through such mechanisms, especially the latter, the Cardenas government instituted some of the most important principles of the Mexican Revolution. The goal of the Revolution for all groups was the creation of a sovereign Mexican State, not subject to foreign control. However, for each group their relationship with the state would vary across time.

All groups understood that for their own interests to be realized, national sovereignty was essential.[11] However, the success of these goals was only partially realized, since Mexico was operating within the restraints of a dependent capitalist position. Cardenas understood the division of Mexican society along class lines and viewed his task as one of conciliation among conflicting classes in the interest of national progress. Cardenas' reforms sought to improve the conditions of peasants and workers so as to create social peace, and a climate of political stability that would permit capitalist development to proceed in Mexico.[12]

Primarily, Cardenas sought to incorporate both peasants (including indigenous groups) and workers into the political and economic system. This, in turn, would help to enhance national sovereignty and strengthen the Cardenas government against mounting opposition. In the case of the peasants, some of the most radical provisions of the Constitution of 1917 were implemented in order to consolidate his support. These were, land reforms, the ejido system, the Ejidal Bank, the CNC (National Confederation of Peasants) and CTM (Confederation of Mexican Workers).[13]

During the 1930s, Cardenas also redistributed thousands of hectares of land in Chiapas, thus establishing the communal ejido system, which provided dozens of Indian communities

35

with their own land. As Collier notes,

> By positioning itself, at least symbolically, as the champion of
> peasants and the poor, the government was able to inspire tremen-
> dous popular support for its programs. Understanding the impor-
> tance of land reform is thus critical in explaining why Chiapas has
> remained a relatively calm area, except for a few outbursts of vio-
> lence during most of the century. When Carlos de Salinas de
> Gortari suspended land reform in 1991, he not only deprived many
> peasants [and indigenous groups] of their hopes of ever farming
> their own land, he also may have compromised the peace that has
> held sway in the countryside for most of this century.[14]

Perhaps one of the most important reforms/developments
under the Cardenas administration was the development of the
corporate party system, or the PRM (Mexican Revolutionary
Party, now referred to as the PRI). Such incorporation is
referred to as the concept of controlled inclusion.[15] Through
the incorporation of key sectors such as labor, peasant and the
popular sector, the party structure "reinforces the state's ideological use of the Mexican revolution to present itself as
defender of the interests of the working class, peasants, and
marginal sectors, and as an opponent of privileged groups and
monopolies."[16] Although authoritarian in nature, the PRM system tended to be inclusive, yet sought state control of these
sectors though its membership. At the same time, the corporatist structure and the institutionalization of the leaders of
popular groups within the party sectors made their incumben-
cy more dependent upon their linkages with the state and party
bureaucracy than with their popular constituencies. The ability of the sectoral structure to convey directly popular will had
been negated; for poor Mexicans this arrangement proved disastrous. The peasant and labor sectors of the official party, the
CNC and the CTM, evolved into pure mechanisms of
control.[17] Thus through the creation of the post-revolutionary
state in Mexico, political and economic control over indigenous groups was established, and through such control the
state was able to keep the indigenous population divided.

The "Indigenous Problem" in Mexico

In the regimes that emerged after the Revolution, the Mexican government classified indigenous peoples in two ways: according to class (economic identity) as peasants or *campesinos*; and according to ethnicity (social identity) as *indigenas*. While the campesinos were the subject of state recognition, the indigenas were the subject of political negation. Revolutionary nationalism made the mestizo the hero of the Revolution, and while Zapata was a revolutionary icon, his Nahua identity was all but forgotten.[18] According to Knight (1990), the campesinos were recognized by the state, however the indigenas were not. Indigenas did, however, become the object of state practices and ideologies; programs were set up to address the indigenous problem.

A corollary that emerges in viewing the indigenous peoples in this context is that the cultural inferiority and backwardness that they are associated with is attributed to themselves as a people, disassociating the socioeconomic dimension. Also, such a perspective suggests that the existence of a large indigenous population with several languages and cultures constituted an obstacle to national unity and progress.[19] The source of the problem according to the Mexican state was cultural. Powell (1996) argues the solution was to incorporate these groups, and under the state's tutelage create a national identity--an identity that left behind the Indian heritage in an effort to create an *imagined* national community in Mexico. Thus the goal of the Mexican government was clear: national cultural homogeneity. This ideally would help address the modern/traditional problem that modernizing nations such as Mexico are facing.[20]

Socioeconomic and cultural assimilation was defined by the state as being in the best interests of indigenous peoples (solving their poverty) and the nation (creating the socioeconomic homogeneity necessary for national development). Thus the Mexican state, as an agent of development, was given the role of representing both the national interest and the indigenous interests. If this project was met with resistance, then it was considered a confirmation of how backward the indigenous groups really were since they were unwilling to work with the progressive state.[21]

In 1948, with the creation of the Indigenous National Institute (INI), the government sought to educate and develop indigenous peoples, as well as further the paternalistic ties between these groups and the state. The INI in Mexico became the channel through which major funding for rural development was administered, making the Indians as clients of the state.[22] Assimilation was the goal, and the INI's first director, Alfonso Caso predicted that the indigenous problem would disappear within 20 years.[23] The impact that the INI had on the identities of several groups was to reinforce and legitimize the racism and existing relations of exploitation and domination in society and the state.[24] In addition, it served to further the institutional marginalization of the indigenous problem from the political arena, from the central agencies of the state, and ultimately isolated them from the resources of the state. Another effect was the separation of Indians from one another:

> By making the INI and corresponding *municipios* the entity through which development programs were channeled, the government helped to unify those within communities while heightening separation between them. As a consequence, Indian communities remained quite isolated and parochial. Indianist programs, furthermore, reinforced the identity of indigenous peoples as Indians rather than as a class of poor rural workers and peasants. Such identity is part of what has led traditionalists in highland communities like Zinacantan and Chamulu, which are closely allied with the PRI to eschew the Zapatistas. In eastern Chiapas, by contrast, the Zapatistas draw upon the shared interests held by peasants and Indians.[25]

Thus the INI was used by the Mexican state as another mechanism of control. By separating the indigenous peoples, the PRI was able to offset the possibility of an Indian movement, thus diminishing the possibility of a truly unified Indian insurrection. This is not to suggest that with such control and stability tensions did not exist; however the Mexican state was in a better position to maintain control and keep the indigenous populations divided, given Mexico's rather stable economic climate up until the crisis of the 1980s.

Economic Restructuring: Understanding the Source of Germinating Tensions.

Since the creation of the autonomous Mexican state after the Revolution of 1910, and the establishment of the corporatist state under Cardenas in the early 1930s, the Mexican government has made several attempts to incorporate indigenous groups into the political process. Such incorporation historically has served as a mechanism for political control, and under the authoritarian state in Mexico, this single party state (PRI) has traditionally been able to maintain a degree of peaceful coexistence among the diverse groups within Mexico. However, drastic political and economic crises in Mexico have upset the delicate balance in society created under the post-revolutionary state.

After the debt crisis hit Latin America in the 1980s, Mexico changed its development strategy. Beginning with the Miguel de la Madrid Administration (1982-1988), Mexico pursued its new economic model. Both Presidents Salinas (1988-1994) and Zedillo (1994-2000) have followed the same neoliberal strategy. As Bresser-Pereira (1993) points out, the "Washington Consensus" holds that fiscal crisis was a direct result of an imbalance between public-sector spending and revenues. The problem, as in many Latin American countries, was that Mexico under the previous ISI model experienced excessive state intervention in the economy. Thus public spending on social services, employment, labor laws, wage regulations, and rent-seeking behavior by domestic industry all created a context that encouraged borrowing to support this intervention, ultimately resulting in a lack of equilibrium in the national economy. In Mexico, addressing the economic crisis has meant undertaking measures to stabilize the economy. This includes: trade liberalization; privatization of state-owned industries; decentralization of the economy; elimination of restrictions on foreign investment (i.e., changes in the foreign investment laws); and flexibilization of labor (which translates into lax labor laws). By following all of these policy prescriptions an attractive environment for foreign investment is created by keeping wages low and investment restrictions at a minimum. Thus the new economic model creates an attractive arena for foreign investment, by allowing for greater efficiency through privatizing previously state-owned sectors of the economy. Once the country is stabilized through austerity measures, privatization and liberalization, new economic growth is thought to be the ultimate result. The idea is that growth comes from private investment in export-oriented industries that take advantage of Mexico's low production costs.[26] The role of the state in the economy is thus redefined, and now a framework is created in which large corporations and transnational capital are the engines of growth.

Mexico's new economic model reflects a shift from an inward-oriented strategy to an export-oriented strategy. This shift in strategy has sent shock waves throughout Mexico, having profound political and economic effects. This is especially true for the indigenous groups in Chiapas who have traditionally relied on the ejido system (communal landholdings), and government restrictions on imports for such crops as corn and subsidies for crops such as coffee. The neoliberal strategy recognizes the displacement of domestic industry, and that the displacement of workers and peasants are all part of the short-term suffering Mexicans must endure in order to improve their well-being in the long run.

The most dramatic changes in the economic sphere came from President Salinas, in respect to the rapid and comprehensive measures he undertook to further his economic agenda. This included relaxing restrictions on foreign investment and tariff reduction. Such reforms, as Gates suggests, were integrated with an overall program of national economic and political modernization, which Salinas claimed were explicitly designed to:

> strengthen Mexico in the global context and improve coexistence among Mexicans to create a viable economy in a strongly competitive international environment and thus to generate employment opportunities for all to forge a more just, more generous, more valuable society for each one of us, more respected in the world..[creating a] democracy with the economic modernization of our country a new political culture.[27]

Thus, in many ways, Salinas presented himself as the savior of Mexico: under his guidance a better and stronger Mexico would emerge.[28]   In 1992, when the Salinas government brought land reform to a halt, it signaled the end of the post-revolutionary ideology. What became apparent was that in Salinas' effort to modernize Mexico, the "backwardness" of the indigenous groups would once again have to be addressed.

Understanding the Zapatista Rebellion

Salinas' claims of modernizing Mexico suggests a specific worldview of modernization. Such meanings attached to the notion of development continue to be those associated with the dominant sectors (global economy). Salinas' liberalizing reforms supported the policy prescriptions of the new world order, which fail to take into account its impact on the Indians and peasants in the modernization process.[29]

In contrast to Salinas and the Mexican state, the Zapatistas have advocated a project of development in which indigenous knowledge and cultures are central rather than peripheral elements, ultimately allowing indigenous communities to govern themselves with political, economic and cultural autonomy. Their position is based on the legacy and ideology of the Revolution, and they specifically address Salinas' drastic changes to Article 27 (land reform) of the Mexican Constitution of 1917. The rural reforms initiated under Salinas had a severe impact on the livelihoods of indigenous groups throughout Mexico and served to undermine essential components of the Revolution. Thus, understanding the manner in which Salinas initiated the reforms highlights how such action functioned as the final blow to the Indians of Chiapas. Indeed, the January 1, 1994 declaration of "hoy decimos basta!" was the battle cry from a group of Indians and peasants who had had enough.

In the Mexican Constitution of 1917, campesinos were accorded economic rights within the agrarian sector. Originally, Article 27 recognized the historic indigenous forms of land tenure and provided grounds for their restitution and the redistribution of new lands in ejidos. Salinas' reform of Article 27 of the Mexican Constitution of the Agrarian Code-- the legislation that made land reform a central tenet of the Mexican economy by eliminating government support of sectors thought to be "anti-modern." The austerity programs dried up subsidies to peasants for fertilizer and other chemical inputs and eroded price supports for crops. According to Collier (1994):

> The de la Madrid's restructuring had stemmed from a paucity of economic resources; Salinas de Gortari's reflected a change of will. Salinas' advisors reached a consensus that Mexico's existing peasantry had to be subjected to major surgery, transformed and absorbed into the modernization of agriculture to increase productivity of millions of peasant-held hectares used for crops but not competitive for world markets, or worked by labor that could be put to more productive use elsewhere. Market subsidies for peasant crops, such as the transport subsidies that the Mexican Coffee Institute had negotiated with the Union of Unions in eastern-Chiapas, had to be eliminated. The entire system of agrarian cred-

its needed to be overhauled, advisors concluded, to circumvent corrupt practices wherein bankers and peasants were colluding in fraudulent claims of crop failure to renege on loans. Furthermore, land reform itself should be brought to a standstill to prevent further land being absorbed into inefficient peasant production. Thus the advisors advocated the privatization and commercialization of peasant and Indian-held parcels.[30]

Under Salinas, the rural restructuring program that formed part of the neoliberal macroeconomic structural adjustment program is represented by the Agrarian Reform Law, directly translating into a reform of Article 27. Rather than overtly eliminating the ejido, the Salinas government moved toward the modernization and transformation of the ejido. The reform to this Article clearly represents an end to the possibility of land redistribution, and specifically counters a major principle of the Revolution. It also reinforces the notion of the dispensability of the rural populations. Moreover, the exclusionary way and speed in which new legislation was formulated demonstrates the institutional marginalization that indigenous groups experience. This also reflects the weakness of the INI within the state apparatus, an organization supposedly created to represent the interest of the indigenous groups. Finally, the Salinas reforms underscore the lack of representationof indigenous interests within the state and the legislative branch.[31]

The rationale behind such rural reforms was to address the shortcomings of agrarian production and increase productivity. The reform also appears to offer greater scope for political intervention in the ejido by changing the internal political dynamics of the ejido and by altering state-ejido relations. The opening of the political structure of the ejido, supposedly to confirm its autonomy, is a mechanism for greater state control, essentially furthering Salinas' neoliberal agenda. Jones suggests that the reform of Article 27 creates new spaces for presidential and federal power through "an invigorated neo-corporatism." While such reforms appear to offer progress along a path to democracy, they actually create a stronger potential for authoritarianism.[32]

Thus the difficulties associated with these reforms may not be obvious upon first glance. Theoretically, increasing productivity in the agrarian sector would appear to bring prosperity to the poorer regions dominated by ejidos. What the Salinas administration attempted to accomplish was to further divide the indigenous groups, by co-opting those who agree to the new neoliberal tenets (private property, individual not communal identity), and granting those groups private property rights to these lands, and alienating those who are less educated, face language barriers and have little knowledge as to how to access information to claim land titles.

Firewood once free for women to gather anywhere in the ejido or communal lands is treated today as a private good to be bought and sold. Now that highland farming requires capital expenditures, poor families without assets more readily rent land to wealthier neighbors. Through changes in Article 27 of the Constitution Salinas and his advisors hope to further liberalize agrarian production. These changes legalize the sharecropping and rental of ejidal lands that have taken place for years. But they also permit unprecedented privatization, mortgaging, the sale of ejidal parcels, and even of formally undivided communal lands. They allow for outside investors to band together with indigenous groups in joint ventures of commercial production based on land. There is no question but that the liberalization of land opens up opportunities for peasants to restructure agrarian production even more than they have already since 1982. But the liberalization also exposes poor and disadvantaged individual peasants to the unprecedented risk of losing land altogether to creditors. It thus removes one more protection for the poor.[33]

The declining economic conditions of the marginalized Indian community was a result of the economic restructuring which is continuing today. The economic hardship suffered by the people of this region was the final blow to the Indians of

Chiapas. Ironically, these reforms have functioned to promote greater unity among indigenous groups. This unity is a result of a dismantled local economy and a repressive state apparatus. Such factors highlight some of the sources of the Zapatista rebellion.

Conclusion: Where Do We Go From Here?

Understanding the impact of multiculturalism, whether it be positive or negative on the maintenance of peaceful coexistence, is a complex issue to address in Mexico or any other region of the world with multicultural societies. The sources of the Chiapas revolt are multifaceted: a reaction to the neoliberal discourses of the government under the Salinas sexenio (1988-1994) in its attempt to abandon much of the discourse of the Revolution, as well as a cry from a civil society that has historically been economically and politically disenfranchised. The recent economic changes in Mexico have, to this point, only furthered the interests of foreign capitalists and elites within the Mexican government and business sectors. The Zapatista rebellion, which was and continues to be a genuinely Indian and peasant rebellion, strikes a blow to the image of the peasant as the thankful beneficiary of the Revolution. These groups have been excluded from the new economic order and are fighting back.

Many scholars (especially economists) argue that the political and economic changes in Mexico have supposedly been for the better. The belief is that Mexico's political system is opening up and that the new economic model being pursued will lead to long-term development. Yet how does one explain the Zapatista rebellion and the hard-line taken by the Mexican government? It is somewhat of a conundrum as to why this modernizing country is taking such a violent stance (as seen in the December 22nd massacre) against indigenous groups which simply ask one thing of their political leaders: to maintain parallel organizations and customary laws within their regions. This request appears to go against Mexico's continued effort to create a new "national identity" while forcing indigenous groups to assimilate, abandoning their cultures and traditions, which are viewed as a hindrance to progress. In the era of neoliberalism, the emphasis on modernization and efficiency pose an even greater threat to indigenous groups, that simply want to preserve their traditions and customary laws.

The uprising of the indigenous forces of the Zapatistas on January 1, 1994 suggests the importance of taking into account indigenous rights. The Salinas' administration's quest to further the interests of Mexico and modernize through the reform of Article 27, which sought to protect the land of indigenous cultures and campesinos through the redistribution of land, contradicts a major principle of the Revolution. Moreover, the government's response to indigenous mobilization and its increasing militarization against the people of Chiapas, reiterates the notion that the indigenous populations continue to be viewed as a problem, essentially subverting their claims to exercise rights as citizens of Mexico.

The structural changes in Mexico have had a direct effect on the lives of indigenous populations, and the Chiapas uprising underscores this phenomenon. The effect of neoliberal reforms, specifically the land tenure reform of Article 27, was that in dismantling the ejido, the government ultimately destroyed the social and economic relations which surrounded it. Neoliberal reform means different things to different groups, and functions to both complement the identities formed around the ideology of the Revolution as in the ranchero communities of Michoacan or clashes as seen in the indigenous populations of Chiapas. In the case of the Zapatistas, this clash has led to demands on the Mexican government to be accountable to those who have been disadvantaged by the growing differentiation in the countryside. As Collier states:

Modernizers need to reconsider whether our societies can afford the impoverization of the masses that accompanies economic restructuring. Corporations pursue cheap labor and hefty profits on a global scale that escapes responsibility for conditions in any given nation. But concentrations of new wealth do not really trickle down to the masses. In the final analysis, can modern economies and modern states afford societies in which so many people are losing their economic power as purchasers and consumers? The Zapatistas are forcing North Americans to ponder this question.[34]

A final element that the Zapatista rebellion underscores is the issue of autonomy, which has been defined by one Indian as:

The capacity to decide not only our own destiny but also more immediate and daily issues, based on our own consciousness and identity. We don't want separation from the Mexican state but are only demanding more liberty to possess, control and administer our territories, to govern our political, economic, social and cultural life, and to participate in national decisions that affect us.[35]

The neoliberal reforms undertaken in Mexico, without consultation or input from those who would be directly impacted, highlight how the indigenous groups (and others, such as workers) are still struggling to govern their political, socioeconomic and cultural life. The massacre on December 22, 1997, also serves as a reminder to the world that the "indigenous problem" has not been resolved, and that the war in Chiapas is far from over. Four years after the Zapatista Army of National Liberation (EZLN) proclaimed war on the Mexican government, the indigenous groups continue to restate their Indian cultural identity.

Perhaps the Mexican government is hoping that the indigenous population, like the international attention it has been receiving, will simply go away. What has emerged in this decade of political and economic change is a new Indian identity that has been constructed and reinforced through their continuous struggle with the Mexican state. This struggle has come to include various ethnic groups against an inflexible state. As Castells (1997) notes,

> On the one hand, they place themselves in historical continuity with five hundred years of struggle against colonization and oppression. On the other hand, they see the reincarnation of this oppression in the current form of the new global order: NAFTA and the liberalizing reforms undertaken by President Salinas, which fail to include the peasants and Indians in the modernization process.[36]

In essence, the Zapatista rebellion reflects the exclusionary consequences of modernization and questions the idea that the only geopolitical order is one which openly embraces capitalism. The rebellion also provides an example of a movement that uses discourses about indigenous rights, democracy and citizenship combined with the ideology of the Revolution, particularly through discourses of the Revolution betrayed by Salinas and the modern Mexican state.[37] Using Emiliano Zapata, the revolutionary leader who fought for the return of communal landholdings to the peasant communities as a key icon, the Zapatistas are staying true to the ideology of the Revolution and its meaning to the indigenous peasant groups that relied on such landholdings for survival. The political and socioeconomic context of multiculturalism in Chiapas, Mexico reflects a struggle between various ethnic Indian groups and the state. A struggle which is far from over.

NOTES

1. Jane Hindley (1995) states that "in 1991 Rigoberta Menchu warned that if governments did not take indigenous rights seriously, then there would be a risk of armed insurrection, such as those that continue to occur in her native village in Guatemala. Menchu's admonition also suggests that violent protests from indigenous peoples are an imminent threat as they continue to learn from the political experience of indigenous groups internationally" (225). The case of Chiapas reflects the idea that Menchu's prediction is indeed valid.
2. Aitken. 1996.
3. "Mestizo" refers to a mix of Spanish and Indian heritage.
4. Aitken. 1996:33

5. Aitken. 1996.

6. Lomintz-Adler. 1992:275-76.

7. Powell. 1996.

8. Middlebrook. 1995:15.

9. Aitken. 1996:28.

10. Lazaro Cardenas (who was a protege of Plutarc Elias Calles) had much in common with Calles, since they had fought together in the Revolution and civil war against Pancho Villa. When Calles rose to power, Cardenas backed him, but the eventual Calles-Cardenas split (which some view in personalistic terms) can be interpreted as an ideological split--the two men stood for different national policies and represented two very different ideological outlooks. See Albert Michaels, 1969. "The Cardenas-Calles Break", in James Wilkie and Albert Michaels (eds.) Revolution in Mexico: Years of Upheaval.

11. How successfully did the Cardenas government carry out the principles of the Revolution? What is clear is that presidential control was essential for the state to carry out the goals of national integration and economic development envisioned by Cardenas. He believed he could guide and direct the process of capitalist development, however, at the same time, dependence on the resources generated through private capital and Mexico's peripheral status limited Mexico's sovereignty. However, through the development of the PRM, his support of peasants and workers, and his attempt to control private and foreign capital, he put forth one of the most important principles of the Mexican revolutionónational sovereignty. The limits to what he could accomplish were due to the structural constraints of the time. Such structural constraints continue to haunt Mexico today. But what remains constant, as the Salinas administration has shown, is the power of the president and his ability to initiate reforms both politically and economically.

12. Hamilton. 1982.

13. Cardenas support for workers is apparent, as Barry (1993) suggests, "Cardenas supported many labor struggles against capital, particularly nationalist conflicts with international capital" (184). His support of labor strikes and labor unification and the development of the National Labor Board also suggest that he was carrying out several of the principles of the revolution.

14. George Collier. 1994:37.

15. Hamilton. 1982:35.

16. Hamilton. 1982:35.

17. Collier. 1994.

18. Hindley. 1995:226.

19. Stavenhagen. 1988.

20. Powell. 1996.

21. Hindley. 1996.

22. Collier. 1994:35.

23. Warman. 1978:143.

24. Hindley. 1996:227.

25. Collier. 1994:110.

26. Barry. 1993:73.

27. Speech from Salinas, quoted in Gates (1996).

28. In addition to the adverse international economic conditions, and pressures from foreign governments, banks and the domestic financial sector, it is also relevant to highlight how the changing environment within the PRI and the government itself. Indeed, despite crisis, it would be difficult to imagine that politicos (politicians) who supported the ISI strategy for years would suddenly make a 180 degree turn in its economic policy. Another dynamic at work during this time was the emergence of the technocrats, who were gaining political clout and ultimately crossing over from financial offices within the Mexican government (e.g., Ministries of Finance and Treasury) to the political forefront including that of the presidency. In Mexico, De la Madrid, Salinas and Zedillo were all cut from the same ideological cloth: neoliberal economic theory. As Moody points out there existed "a strong political resurgence of the technocratic factions associated with the Treasury and the Central Bank, a sharply diminished role for the politicos connected with the PRI and the labor movement, and the virtual elimination of structuralist and neo-Keynsian economists from top levels of government". These technocrats, usually economists, with advanced degrees from Harvard and Yale sought to create a leaner, more efficient and technocratic form of authoritarian rule, one that was compatible with the neoliberal agenda. The new type of politicians emerging in the 1980s and 1990s consider themselves the modernizers of Mexico. Salinas continually referred to himself as the "modernizer" of Mexico. Unlike the dinosaurs of the past, the technocrats, such as Salinas are espousing a neoliberal agenda, and such modernizers play a crucial role in introducing and carrying out Mexico's new economic model. This of course, carries implications for the indigenous peoples who were thought to be a hindrance to modernization.

29. Castells. 1997:77.

30. Harvey. 1995:204.

31. Rural reform, specifically the reform of Article 27, is a generic term to describe three related pieces of legislation. This includes the new Article 27 of the Mexican Constitution, the new Agrarian Law and the new Agrarian Law regulations. Together, they establish four changes. First, they enhance autonomy of decision making of the Asemblea General (general assembly of ejidatarios in a community). Second, they establish the right to convert land use rights into individual parcels in a market restricted to ejidatarios; subsequent land sales will treat the parcels as private property and require the authorization of a notary public and a formal valuation. Prior to the 1991 constitutional reform, agrarian reform beneficiaries (ejidatarios) could not legally sell or rent their land-use rights, and many other forms of economic activity were constrained by government regulation. Third, they promote the right to transfer the ejido land to private companies for up to 30 years or set up joint partnerships, including foreign firms. Fourth, they establish new methods of land tenure regularization. See Jones (1996).

32. Jones. 1996:203.

33. Collier. 1994:124.

34. *Interhemispheric Resource Bulletin.* 1996:5.

35. Adelfo Regino. 1996:6. *Interhemispheric Resource Bulletin.*

36. Castells. 1997:77.

37. Castells. 1997.

REFERENCES

Aitken, R. 1996. "Neoliberalism and Identity: Redefining State and Society in Mexico", in Aitken, Craske, and Jones (eds.) *Dismantling the Mexican State?* London: Macmillan Press.

Barry, Tom. 1993. *Mexico: A Country Guide*. Albuquerque, NM: Interhemispheric Research Center:

Branch, H.N. 1927. *The Mexican Constitution*. Washington: Government Printing Office.

Bresser-Pereira, Luiz Carlos; Maravall, Jose, and Pezeworski, Adam (eds) 1992. *Economic Reforms in New Democracies*. Cambridge: Cambridge University Press.

Bulmer-Thomas, Victor, ed. 1996. *The New Economic Model in Latin America and It's Impact on Income Distribution and Poverty*. New York: St. Martin's Press.

Cameron, Maxwell A. 1992. "Micro and Macro Logic of Political Conflict". In Archibald Ritter, Maxwell Cameron and David Pollock eds. *Latin America to the Year 2000*. New York, NY: Praeger Press.

Castells, Manuel. 1997. *The Power of Identity*. Malden, MA: Blackwell Publishers.

Collier, George. 1994. *Basta!: Land and the Zapatista Rebellion in Chiapas*. Oakland: Food First Books.

Cook, M. Middlebrook, K. and Horcasitas, J. eds. 1994. *The Politics of Economic Restructuring*. La Jolla: Center for U.S.-Mexican Studies (UCSD).

Cornelius, W., Craig, A. and Fox, J. eds. 1994. *Transforming State Society Relations in Mexico: The National Solidarity Strategy*. La Jolla: Center for U.S-Mexican Studies (UCSD).

Craske, N. 1996. "Dismantling or Retrenchment? Salinas and Corporatism", in Aitken, Craske, and Jones (eds.) *Dismantling the Mexican State?* London: Macmillan Press.

De la Garza Toledo, E. "The Restructuring of State-Labor Relations in Mexico", in Cook, Middlebrook, and Horcasitas, (eds.). *The Politics of Economic Restructuring*. La Jolla: Center for U.S-Mexican Studies (UCSD).

Diamond, Larry, Linz, Juan and Seymar, M., 1995. *Politics in Developing Countries*. Boulder, CO; Lynne Reinner.

Dresser, D. 1994. "Embellishment, Empowerment, or Euthanasia of the PRI?", in Cook, Middlebrook, and Horcasitas, (eds). *The Politics of Economic Restructuring*. La Jolla: Center for U.S-Mexican Studies (UCSD).

51

Dresser, D. 1991. "Neopopulist Solutions to Neoliberal Problems: Mexico's National Solidarity Program", in Cornelius, Craig and Fox (eds.) *Transforming State Society Relations in Mexico: The National Solidarity Strategy.* La Jolla: Center for U.S-Mexican Studies (UCSD).

Foley, Michael W. 1995. "Debt, Democracy and Neoliberalism in Latin America." In M. Dorraj, ed. *The Changing Political Economy of the Third World.* Boulder, CO: Lynne Reiner.

Fox, J. 1993. "The Difficult Transition from Clientelism to Citizenship: Lessons from Mexico," *World Politics.*

Fox, J. 1994. "Political Change in Mexico's New Peasant Economy", in Cook, Middlebrook, and Horcasitas, (eds). *The Politics of Economic Restructuring.* La Jolla: Center for U.S-Mexican Studies (UCSD).

Gates, Marilyn. 1996. "The Debt Crisis and Economic Restructuring", in Otero, ed, *Neoliberalism Revisited.* Boulder, CO: Westview Press.

Haber, P. 1994. "The Art and Implications of Political Restructuring in Mexico", in Cook, Middlebrook, Horcasitas, (eds.), *The Politics of Economic Restructuring.* La Jolla: Center for U.S-Mexican Studies (UCSD).

Hamilton, Nora. 1982. *The Limits of State Autonomy in Mexico.* University of Nebraska Press.

Harvey, N. 1995. *Rebellion in Chiapas.* La Jolla: Center for US-Mexico Relations (UCSD).

Hewlege, Ann. 1994. "Stabilization Policy in Latin America: Debates About Growth and Distribution". In G. Bird and A. Hewlege eds. *Latin America's Economic Future.* New York, NY: Harcourt, Brace & Co.

Hindley, Jane. 1996. "Towards a Pluralcultural Nation: The limits to Article 4", in Aitken, Craske, and Jones (eds.) *Dismantling the Mexican State?* London: Macmillan Press.

Horcasitas, Juan. 1997. "Changing the Balance of Power in a Hegemonic Party System: The Case of Mexico", in Lijphart and Waisman, eds. *Institutional Design In New Democracies.* Boulder, CO: Westview Press.

Interhemisheric Resource Center Bulletin. 1996. *Mexico's New Indian Movement.* Albuquerque, NM: University of New Mexico.

Jones, Gareth. 1996. "Dismantling the Ejido: A Lesson in Controlled Pluralism", in Aitken, Craske, and Jones (eds.) *Dismantling the Mexican State?* London: Macmillan Press.

Klesner, J. 1994. "Realignment or Dealignment? Consequences of Economic Crisis and

Restructuring for the Mexican Party System", in Cook, Middlebrook, and Horcasitas, (eds). *The Politics of Economic Restructuring.* La Jolla: Center for U.S-Mexican Studies (UCSD).

Knight, A. 1990. "Racism, Revolution and Idnigenismo", in R. Graham, (ed.) *The Idea of Race in Latin America.* Austin: University of Texas Press.

Knight, A. 1996. "Salinas and Social Liberalism in Historical Context" in Aitken, Craske, and Jones (eds.) *Dismantling the Mexican State?* London: Macmillan Press.

Lawton, J. ed. 1995. *Privatization Amidst Poverty.* Boulder, CO: Lynne Reinner.

Lomitz-Adler, C. 1992. *Exits from the Labyrinth. Culture and Ideology in the Mexican National Space.* Berkeley: University of California Press.

Lopez, B. 1994. "Los derechos indigenas en Mexico y el convenio 169" (Indigenous Rights in Mexico and the International Convention 169). *Ojarassca,* 33-4:pp43-6.

Lustig, Nora. 1995. *Coping with Austerity.* Washington D.C.: Brookings Institute.

Maddison, A. 1992. *The Political Economy of Poverty, Equality and Growth: Brazil and Mexico.* Oxford University Press.

Mainwaring, Scott and Shugart, Matthew. 1997. *Presidentialism in Latin America.* Cambridge, MA: Cambridge University Press.

Menchu, Rigoberta. 1991. *I, Rigoberta Menchu: An Indian Women in Guatemala.* Edited by Elisabeth Burgos-Debray. London: Verso Books.

Middlebrook, Kevin. 1996. *The Paradox of Revolution.* Baltimore, MD. Johns Hopkins University Press.

Moody, Kim. 1995 "Nafta and the Corporate Redesign of North America," *Latin American Perspectives,* 22:1; pp. 95-115.

Morley, Samuel. 1995. *Poverty and Inequality in Latin America.* Baltimore: Johns Hopkins University Press.

Otero, Gerardo, ed. 1996. *Neoliberalism* Revisited. Boulder, CO: Westview Press.

Phillip, George, ed. 1993. "The New Economic Liberalism and Democracy in Latin America: Friends or Enemies?" *Third World Quarterly* 14(3):555-561.

Powell, Kathy. 1996. "Neoliberalism and Nationalism", in Aitken, Craske, and Jones (eds.) *Dismantling the Mexican State?* London: Macmillan Press.

Rodriguez, Jaime. 1993. *The Evolution of the Mexican Political System.* Wilmington Delaware:SR Books.

Roett, Riordan. 1995. *The Challenge of Institutional Reform in Mexico.* Boulder, CO:

Lynne Reinner.

Smith, William, Acuna, Carlos and Gamarra, Eduardo. Eds. 1994. *Democracy, Markets, and Structural Reform in Latin America.* New Brunswick: Transaction Publishers.

Stavenhagen, R. 1988. Derecho Indigena y Derecho Humanos en America Latina. Mexico: Colegio de Mexico and Instituto Americano de Derechos Humanos.

Varley, A. 1996. "Delivering the Goods: Solidarity, Land Regulation and Urban Services," in Aitken, Craske, and Jones (eds.) Dismantling the Mexican State? London: Macmillan Press.

Weldon, Jeffrey. 1997. "Political Sources of Presidencialismo", in Mainwaring and Shugart (eds.) Presidentialism in Latin America. Cambridge, MA: Cambridge University Press.

CHAPTER III

MULTICULTURALISM IN THE UNITED STATES
Sylvia Whitlock, Ph.D.*

Culture consists of all those things people have learned to do, believe, value and enjoy in their history. It is the ideals, beliefs, skills, tools, customs and institutions into which each member of society is born. Human and cultural diversity are important factors which merit increased sensitivity and awareness.

> We have an obligation to meet in our society, one we should start by giving the students in our schools an understanding and appreciation of the racial, ethnic, and cultural diversity of California and the United States, so as to reinforce each student's sense of dignity and self-worth, whatever his origin. To accomplish this task, we must start with teachers and other school staff to make them competent to impart such understanding and appreciation. They must be well-informed regarding the history, culture and current problems of diverse ethnic groups; and they must relate effectively to those subjects and to the different groups of children who make up the student body of their schools. When there is general understanding and appreciation of racial, ethnic, cultural, national origins and religious diversity, we will come closer to achieving the ideal of equal opportunity in a multicultural society.

So spoke Wilson Riles, Superintendent of Education in the State of California, when in March 1973, 25 years ago, California embarked on an ambitious program to address multiculture. Multicultural Education, not yet conceived of as an interdisciplinary process, was received with mixed reviews. That the cognitive aspect of the training seemed to outweigh the affective did nothing to dispel the resistance evident in staff

---

* Sylvia Whitlock is a practicing psychotherapist and curriculum consultant. She holds a Ph.D. from Claremont Graduate University.

reactions. The major problem, the most difficult to tackle was that of attitude change. Webster defines attitude as "the manner of acting, feeling or thinking that shows one's disposition, opinion, etc. Attitudes are shaped by experiences and may be manipulated or modified through experiences."

The reality of life in a small tropical island, originally inhabited by Arawak Indians, illustrates the socialization process with which education has, through the centuries, been associated. This mecca of colonial slave traders, dealing in human merchandise from Africa, was inhabited during the thirties and forties by a numerical majority population of working class blacks and a minority population of ruling class colonists from Great Britain. In this environment it was difficult for participants in the educational structures to distinguish or even perceive a difference between class structure and racial structures.

In such an environment I spent the formative years of my childhood, with nary an awareness of racial identity, but decided sensitivity to the color of a person's skin. It was a foregone conclusion that to be poor and dark skinned was to be without any redeeming graces whatsoever. Money, if one had an abundance of it, could be used to buy acceptance and prestige. Society, however, conferred its favors first on the winning combination of alabaster skin and fortune fair.

Before the "Ugly American" began to bear the burden of his country's foreign and domestic policy, an American accent, in the eyes of the unsophisticated islanders, was a desirable asset almost in the ranking category of fair skin and fortune. Ambitious parents, who saw the promised land of America as the place to earn a fortune but not to spend it, sent their children back to the islands to assure them upbringings free of the tensions of urban America.

My childhood was completely free of racial incidents. I

was twenty years old and in America before I experienced the trauma of rejection because of my racial identification, and then it was so carefully and explicitly defined as to leave no doubt as to the reasons for the exclusion. Since this exclusion was not characteristic of the profile of social relationships in my island, I developed a naivete about the many and varied manifestations of racial prejudice. This persisted well into my adult years; building up a sophisticated response to the reality of the American dilemma and all its ugly ramifications has been painful but inescapable.

Allport says the context of a child's learning is always the social structure in which his personality develops. My childhood experiences shaped two significant aspects of my personality. I grew up secure in the feeling that my own abilities and efforts would see me through. It never occurred to me that the color of my skin could be a hindrance, although I did not lack a prejudicial response to the various colors of skin that was at the same time qualitative in its applications. The psychodynamics of that response are clearly identifiable in the subtle forms of prejudice and scorn that were part of my early experiences in school and society, experiences carefully nurtured and reinforced by teachers and family. The emergent aspect of my personality, however, was a positive self-concept. The second aspect was the incredible denial of the destructive and widespread existence of prejudice and an implicit belief in the ultimate fairness of human beings. This aspect has been modified extensively by the reality of my experience in these United States, almost to the point of reconstruction. What remains is an appreciation that the one aspect has equipped me to deal with the other.

So where are we in our attitude adjustment? Oppression of minorities is not a thing of the past. Indeed, from a current perspective it seems that many of the gains made in the 70s have leveled off or are sliding backwards as we approach the close of this millennium. Legislative and judicial achievements of the 60s and the 70s came under attack in the 80s and 90s. Things are never even in situations where people must interact and interplay. In an attempt to strive for such evenness, we have discarded the knowledge that we all have started in different places on the track and we are making moves which deny the existence of curves around the track. Racial and ethnic minorities continue to experience discrimination in housing, employment, and education. Physical harassment and abuse of minorities continue to rise.

There is a large income gap between very wealthy (mostly European Americans) and the very poor (disproportionately composed of America's racial minorities). Historically, the US has promoted the "melting pot" image that was even dramatized in the play "The Melting Pot" by British playwright Israel Zangwill, performed here first in 1908. Not all thinkers have subscribed to this image. Gladys Baker of the University of Michigan preferred to describe the culturally pluralistic image as one of a mosaic, where all pieces contributed to the whole but each piece retained its uniqueness and was not "melted down". Others opposed the theory for different reasons. The Chinese Exclusion Act, passed by Congress in 1862, was the first of a number of federal and state laws established to insure that certain immigrant groups would have minimal impact on the emerging American culture. In 1926, Henry Pratt Fairchild, a noted sociologist, wrote that "the melting pot philosophy and unrestricted immigration were slowly, insidiously, irresistibly eating away the very heart of the United States." The heart of the US was defined as an American culture that was based primarily on the values and mores of early immigrants, principally English, Irish, German and Scandinavian groups. Instead of melting all groups, including Americans, it was proposed that, to reduce the effects of the melting pot phenomenon and to increase the probability of cultural assimilation, immigration quotas be developed for those countries whose culture diverged most from the American culture.

The conflict of cultures is like any other conflict. The resolution of a conflict situation requires more than an awareness that it exists. If self-insight is not operative and people are unaware of conflicts or prejudices, then resolution of the problems requires a variety of sensitive approaches.

Allport describes "repression" as another means of dealing with conflict:

> In almost every community where the subject of prejudice or discrimination is brought up the first response is, "Here we have no problem." The mayor's office will make this assertion, so will the man in the street in villages and cities, in North and in South... it may be that they are so accustomed to the familiar caste and class lines that they regard them as normal... no one wants to be at odds with his own conscience. Man has to live with himself. He finds it uncomfortable to admit that malintegration exists within his character. It is not surprising, then, to hear the statement, "I have no prejudices", even when an outsider sees them bristling.

When these prejudices are present in institutional systems dedicated to the education of youth, they represent a conflict between the American creed, the Judeo-Christian beliefs, and practice. It has been traditional in America that social policy changes be mandated by law. Traditions die hard nonetheless.

Let's look at some of the larger groups which make up our communities today.

African Americans

Black culture is a people-rather than a thing-oriented culture. It places an important emphasis on humanism. This situation occurs despite typical Saturday night rows that claim African American (AA) lives or the infiltration of drugs into AA communities. Such occurrences have distressed more AAs than whites because these factors indicate the destruction of minority lives and their communities. America enjoys probably the highest standard of living in the world. It has not been gained without cost. African Americans, historically isolated from the mainstream, have been unable to resist the allure of this movement, pushing onward through the end of this millennium and into the next. They are however, more spectators than participants. Within the black culture, there are broad ranges of behavior as well as important class and geographic distinctions that may be observed among members of this cultural group. Along such lines, Gordon in 1964 made a useful distinction regarding the cultural perspectives of African Americans. According to him, there are two types of identities AA share, the historical and the participational. The historical definition refers to AA's development as a race and their sense of peoplehood. The participational definition centers around the behavior similarities they may share. With a person of the same class, but a different ethnic group, one shares a sense of peoplehood. With those of the same ethnic but different social class, one shares the sense of peoplehood but not behavioral similarities, the only criterion which meets both these criteria are people of the same ethnic and social class. There are forces that have historically estranged blacks and whites giving rise to lack of trust, the prejudices surrounding cultural differences **and subtle** and overt forms of racial discrimination. The objective conditions confronting the majority of persons of African ancestry are still predominately those of poverty, limited employment, thwarted educational opportunities and overt/covert acts of racism.

Some individual AA have benefitted from employment opportunities in professions not available to their predecessors. Swinton states that, "in fact, there has been an increase in the proportion of AA who can be classified as upper middle class." No people, however have ever been judged by the condition of its exceptions. Martin Luther King said, "it was the negro who educated the nation to the brutal facts of segregation by dramatizing the evils through non-violent protest. Social scientists have played little or no role in disclosing the truth about AA or other minorities."

The history of AA is the struggle of a people to survive against great odds and injustices. It is both the bond that welds them together and sets them apart from other Americans. If one can speak of AAs as a homogenous group, they have experienced a cultural press different from that experienced by many minority groups in America. Few ethnic or racial minorities in American society have been so thoroughly blocked from having a constructive identity group formation, have been pressed to trust whites more so than themselves, have had a value system imposed on them that so totally and forcefully undermined their self esteem and their very existence. W.E.B. DuBois noted, "Prolonged policies of segregation and discrimination have involuntarily welded the mass almost into a nation within a nation, with its own schools, churches, hospitals, newspapers and many business enterprises." The common bond that unites AA is not the color of their skins (for their colors vary) but rather the experiences they have collectively and individually been forced to endure because of their skin color. The children born to the young adults of the mid 60s and 70s have reached adulthood. They grew up in a sociocultural environment that, for the most part, abandoned the overt, brutal manifestation of oppression, such as lynchings, public humiliation, and blatant discrimination. The rhetoric of equal opportunity, affirmative action, and full rights of citizenship served as palliatives to mask the persistent, institutionalized racism and oppression. If one can speak of a people as an acting entity, it was as though there was a collective sigh of relief and a generation accepted the illusion of equal opportunity and equality as real.

The ability to confront the unadulterated truth with resolve and fortitude, together with spirituality and humaneness and love of life, has been part of the unique heritage of African Americans. The quest of modernism and desire for assimilation at all costs is a denial of these. The humanism of AAs is also evident in family situations. Few Black women give up out of wedlock children for adoption. Instead, within the community, children are treated usually with little distinction regarding the legitimacy or illegitimacy of their birth, even though out-of-wedlock pregnancies are not condoned. The humanistic orientation is also supported by studies of their vocational interests and choices. In his 1965 study of the vocational interests of black and white 9th graders, Chansky found that while minority youth were interested in interpersonal, business, verbal and long term training occupations, white youth were interested in occupations that had high prestige rather than ones that related to their own true interests. Likewise, Bayer and Boruch found that minority people were more likely to choose social occupations than were whites. (Observation in Ebony Magazine among female students). History suggests that strong family ties bounded families together during the confusion that followed the Civil War. They have developed an ability to persevere and succeed despite the odds.

Latino Community

The term Hispanic is gradually replacing the synonym Latino, which was defined as a generic label including all people of Spanish origin and descent, and preferred by some Hispanics because it stresses their Latin American background. They are members of a single culture group in the sense that they share a fairly common history. Spaniards arrived in the New World in the early 16th Century and brought with them a fairly European homogeneous culture. The conquest of Mexico was followed by exploration and colonization. By the middle of the 16th Century, the original immigrants from Spain, native Indians from Mexico, and their mestizo children had founded permanent settlements in northern New Mexico. This process continued and soon all of the area known today as the Southwest was settled. Hispanic Latino communities are diverse and heterogeneous. Many of these communities continue to be plagued by sociocultural, health, emotional and environmental problems. According to the 1985 census, the proportion of Hispanic families below the poverty level was more than double that of non-Hispanic families. Hispanic group's intradiversity is also noted, with Puerto Rican families having the highest poverty rate and Cubans the lowest. There is substantial immigration to the United States from Spanish-speaking countries. Many legal and undocumented individuals come in from Mexico, Central America and the Caribbean. The Latin American refugee population deserves special attention. Increasing numbers of immigrants are arriving from Central American countries, particularly El Salvador and Nicaragua. Their profile tends to be different from other Latino groups in the United States. Many of them are considered political refugees from ongoing civil wars. Their experiences differ from those of other Latinos, many of whom are political exiles (Cuba, Chile) and not displaced persons who tend to come from a lower socio-economic background. The political exile tends to be more educated and resourceful, has made a choice, being fully aware of its consequences, and usually has made some arrangement and established some support in the United States.

I mentioned before that many Latino communities experience socioeconomic, health and psychosocial problems. AIDS among Latino communities is high. Needed are community efforts to incorporate strategies for the development of appropriate educational materials which are culturally sensitive. Education represents the most serious gap in achievement between Latinos and other groups, ranging from preschool through graduate training levels. It continues to be a serious problem for Puerto Rican and Mexican Americans. The median number of years of formal schooling for males 25 years and older is as follows: Hispanics 9.3 yrs., general population 12.2 yrs. and Blacks 9.6 yrs. The number of Americans who have completed five years of school or less breaks down by ethnicity as follows: Hispanics 19.5%, general population 5.0% and

Blacks 13.5%. The data on graduation from high school are: Hispanic 32.6%, general population 56.4%, Blacks 34.7%. Clearly, Latinos are a significantly undereducated group, compared both to the general population and to Afro-Americans. With education so limited it should come as no surprise to find that Latinos are overrepresented in occupations that are menial and low paid. Latino unemployment is significantly higher than that of Anglos though not as high as that of Afro-Americans.

The ability to speak English has been linked to Latino school achievement. The social and political pressure to discontinue bilingual education is well-documented here in California. Indeed the polls have addressed what is a growing discontent with the needy condition of many Latinos, focusing especially on undocumented individuals. Although they reside in every state, Latinos tend to be urban and to be concentrated in the Southwestern, Southeastern and Northeastern areas of the United States. They are diverse in ethnicity, socioeconomic class, color, geographic distribution, generational status, degree of acculturation and language preference. Despite centuries of voluntary acculturation, Latinos in the US have retained Spanish fluency and other traditions of Hispanic culture. Furthermore, Spanish fluency and the Latino culture have survived centuries of involuntary acculturation, such as the English Only rule that characterized the educational system of the Southwest for a long time and now threatens again. The majority of Hispanics are bicultural in the sense that they are members of both the Hispanic and Anglo cultures. The range of commitment to the Anglo and Hispanic cultures varies widely. Some are very Hispanic and some are very Anglo and most are at various points between the extremes. An important cultural value ingrained in the traditional family is respect. It governs all positive reciprocal interpersonal relationships dictating the appropriate deferential behavior toward others on the basis of age, socioeconomic position, sex and authority status. The lowest common denominator of cultural sensitivity with

Latinos is generally that of linguistic accessibility.

Asian Americans

As the number of Asian Americans increases, greater attention is being paid to the impact of culture conflicts between Asian and European values. The number of Asian and Pacific Island Americans is projected to reach ten million by the beginning of the next millennium. Much of this is due to the relaxation of the immigration laws. The influx of Asians has changed the character of the Asian population in the US. With the exception of the Japanese, most Asian groups are now comprised of internationally born individuals. Because of this large increase in the Asian population, greater attention needs to be placed on the impact of culture clash and racism on the development of the Asian American identity. In contrast to many Third World groups, the image of Asian Americans is that of a highly successful minority who have "made it" in society. A close analysis of the census seems to support this. The Chinese and Japanese in this country have exceeded the national median income, and even Filipinos who lagged behind almost through the 60s have now attained parity.

A more striking indication of "success" is the apparent reduction of social distance between Asians and whites. The Bogardus Social Distance Scale, a measure of prejudice and or discrimination against minority groups, documents the incidence of marrying and forming intimate relations with the dominant group. The incidence of interracial marriage for Japanese Americans for areas like Los Angeles, Fresno and San Francisco has approached 50%. They are extremely high among Japanese and Filipino youth. Black/White marriages for the same period was well under 2%. These data are ironic in light of the massive discrimination that, historically, has been directed at Asians. Unknown to the general public, Asian Americans have been the object of much prejudice and discrimination. Ironically, the American public, for the most part, is unaware that higher walls of prejudice have been raised around Asians than any other ethnic minority. They have been denied the rights of citizenship, denied ownership of land, assaulted, murdered, and placed in concentration camps during World War II. Asians have, however, generally attempted to function in the existing society without loud, strong, public protests. Recent attempts to right those wrongs have had mixed reception in the community at large. A discussion of Asian cultural values is difficult since Asian and Pacific Islanders are made up of more than twenty-five distinct groups. The first Chinese immigrants came to the US in the 1840s to escape social and economic unrest in their country. There was a great demand here for Chinese help to build the trans-continental railroad. They were "cheap labor" and as such were welcomed into the work force. However, a diminishing labor market made the immigrants no longer welcome because of fear of the "yellow peril." Their pronounced racial and cultural differences from the white majority made them conspicuous and they served as scapegoats for the resentment of white workers. This anti-Chinese sentiment culminated in the passing of the Federal Chinese Exclusion Act of 1882 which was the first immigration exclusion act against any ethnic group. The Japanese in America also faced severe hostility and discrimination from white citizens. They had begun to immigrate to the US during the 1890s when anti-Chinese sentiment was great. As a result, they shared in the pervasive Anti-Asian feelings. Originally brought in to fill the demand for cheap agricultural labor and coming from an agrarian background, many Japanese became engaged in these fields. Their fantastic success in the agricultural occupations, coupled with a racist climate, enraged many white citizens. Legislation, similar to the anti-Chinese acts was passed against the Japanese. Against this background, it became relatively easy for society to accept the relocation of 110,000 Japanese Americans into camps during World War II. Today, many people perceive that obstacles no longer exist. *Time, US News and World Report,* and *Newsweek* have often described Asians as a "model minority", successful and functioning well in society. Such articles downplay the problems faced by Asians. Studies of Indochinese refugees indicate they suffer more psychological problems than found in the general population. Over one-third of the Vietnamese and two-thirds of the Hmong and Laotian refugees have family incomes below the poverty level. Many have run across subtle and indirect prejudice and discrimination. They are underrepresented in managerial positions, and although advances have been made, it is still apparent that social and economic discrimination is being practiced against Asian Americans.

Values of filial piety, modesty and restraint of emotions are important to Asian American groups. However the dominant culture which values independence and assertiveness often views Asian values negatively and as deficits. Kitano believes that Asian Americans can be classified along four dimensions of acculturation: 1. High Assimilation and Low Ethnic Identity individuals who identify primarily with Western values and have little identification with their ethnic culture, 2. Low Assimilation, Low Ethnic Identity, truly marginal individuals, who do not have a sense of identity with either culture, 3. High Assimilation, High Ethnic Identity- bicultural with the ability to accept both cultural systems, and 4. Low Assimilation, High Ethnic Identity made up mostly of recent immigrants and refugees. They want to remain close to traditional values and keep contact with outsiders to a minimum.

The major Asian American groups have done very well academically in the US. A greater number of Asians complete high school than that found in the total US population and twice as many complete four years of college. They score highly on achievement tests but tend to score less so on the verbal areas of aptitude tests. They are over-represented in the most prestigious universities, many of which are beginning to place barriers to the admission of Asian American students.

Many groups within this culture however, remain undereducated. There are four times as many Chinese and Filipinos with fewer than four years education when compared to Caucasians in the US. Certain groups of Asians and Pacific Islanders show a less than 50% completion of high school: Hmong-22.3; Laotians-31.4; Cambodians-42.6. The factors involved in the low achievement of these groups merit some study. The reason for academic success of most Asian Americans is a matter of speculation. Some feel that the promotion of academic achievement within the Asian culture is an important factor; others think that education is perceived as an avenue of advancement when other areas are closed. It is also possible that a combination of cultural values and societal access are involved in the academic success of Asian Americans. An abundance of Asian American students enter the Physical Sciences, approximately 75% of males and 54% of females. Asians prefer structured rather than ambiguous tasks.

Occupations that require verbal assertion may conflict with the value of restraint in expression. There is greater acceptance and understanding of science. Among Southeast Asian refugees and immigrants, career plans that are acceptable to parents involve medicine, dentistry, teaching and pharmacy. Those that have less acceptance are art, music and writing. Career plans for Asian Americans merit some scrutiny because of the fear of having their choices limited by prejudice and discrimination. For Asian Americans, the family can be an extremely important point of reference as a microcosm of cultural heritage and identity. People seek help from their families first. Western culture almost invariably values independence. Dependence, on the other hand, is a key concept applicable to human relations in many Asian countries. Sensitivity and awareness of differences can contribute to bringing about a new state of balance.

An ostrich-like stance still pervades with reference to multiculture. Solution procedures must be interdisciplinary and address themselves to developing both cognitive and affective modes. There are two distinct aspects of multicultural education which need to be considered. One involves preparation of teachers to understand and meet the need for this concept in education; the other is the process which should be part of the content of every youngster's experiences. There is a basic assumption that the persons involved in the education of today's youngsters represent a microcosm of today's society, with all its characteristics intact. Terence Tice, in a discussion of multicultural objectives, said they were shaped by myths about multicultural education. He saw schools, as they moved out of the private arena into public obligation, assuming functions that tended to perpetuate the status quo. Thus, education, in maintaining the social system, was inefficient in recognizing or placing positive values on diversity. Ponterotto and Casas, 1991, advanced a model of cultural diversity which makes several assumptions: First and foremost is the explicit belief that to be culturally different does not equate with deviancy or inferiority. Second, there is strong acknowledgement that racially ethnic minorities are bicultural and function in at least two different cultural contexts. Third, biculturality is seen as a positive and desirable quality which enhances the full range of human potential.

In today's shrinking world, where the reality of international communication and commerce is only a keypad away, social status is in the eye of the beholder. Our common humanity assumes gigantic proportions with boundless implications for the need for affective growth.

Knowledge of another person's historical and cultural background alone does not guarantee insight or understanding. Each individual is like all the other people, like some other people and like no other person. In this cosmopolitan arena called America we must respond responsibly and with integrity to the reality of cultural pluralism.

Bibliography

Human Resources Division (1990) *Asian Americans: A Status Report.* Washington, D.C. U.S. General Accounting Office.

Zane, W.S., Sue, S., Hu, L-T., & K, J-H. (1991). Asian American Assertion: A social learning analysis of cultural diffences. *Journal of Counseling Psychology,* 38, 63-70.

U.S. Committee for Refugees (1987). *World Refugee Survey;* 1986 in reviews. Washington, D.C.: American Council for Nationalities Service.
Allport, G. (1958) *The Nature of Prejudice,* New York: Doubleday, Anchor Books.

Schaefer, R.T. (1988). *Racial and Ethnic Groups.* Glenview, II: Scott-Foresman.

McAdoo, H. (1988) The Study of Ethnic Minority Families: Implication for Practitioners and Policymakers. *Family Relations.* 37 265-267.

Leslie, L.A. & Leitch, M.L. (1989). A Demographic Profile of Recent Central American Immigrants: *Hispanic Journal of Behavioral Science,* 11(4), 315-329.

Whitelock, Sylvia. Ph.D. Dissertation, 1978. Claremont Graduate University.

CHAPTER IV

MODEL COUNTRIES OF
MULTICULTURAL COEXISTENCE
Thomas Greene, Ph.D.*

American Politics and Racial Division

1988. The last year of Ronald Reagan's presidency. As in the case of the previous two-term Republican president (Dwight Eisenhower), the Republican party's leadership falls more by default than by design to the incumbent vice president, George Bush (in 1960, Richard Nixon).

Democrats, out of the White House for the last eight years and for sixteen of the last twenty years, joyfully contemplate George Bush's vulnerabilities and line up to compete for the Democratic party's presidential nomination--except for New York governor Mario Cuomo, arguably the Democrats' strongest presidential candidate. Governor Cuomo is content to let his Democratic competitors bump each other off in the party's presidential primaries so that he then can step forward at convention time, unbloodied and untarnished, to claim the party's nomination. It seemed a good plan at the time. The story of the bumping off process of the 1988 Democratic presidential competition is summarized in the following table.

1988 Democratic Presidential Primary Elections:
Percentage Vote, by Candidate

	NH (2-16)	Super Tues. (3-8)	IL (3-15)	MI (3-26)	CT (3-29)	NY (4-19)	PA (4-26)
Dukakis	36	26	17	28	59	51	67
Gephardt	20	13	-	13	-	-	-
Gore	7	26	-	2	8	10	4
Jackson	8	27	33	55	27	37	28
Simon	17	2	42	2	1	-	-
Jackson	44	53	50	83	86	88	95

* Thomas Greene is Associate Professor of Political Science, University of Southern California. He holds a Ph.D. from Cornell University.

The cold numbers in the table remind us of the heat of the competition at the time. Michael Dukakis, governor of Massachusetts, starts fast in February in neighboring New Hampshire, slumps until the end of March, but has the nomination wrapped up by the end of April, well before convention time. Governor Cuomo is left lying in the dust without ever having crossed the starting line. What happened?

The Reverend Jesse Jackson happened. Jesse Jackson-- attractive, articulate, committed, perhaps a genuine example of charismatic leadership in American politics, and Jesse Jackson--African-American. In the New Hampshire primary, and in the sixteen mainly southern primaries of Super Tuesday, Jackson is an unknown quantity and is only a minor irritant to the other candidates. But in the Illinois primary, and especially in the Michigan primary, Jesse Jackson explodes onto the scene as a highly credible candidate who might win enough delegates in the primaries to be Number One going into the party's national convention. Alarm bells ring all along the Democratic party's corridors of power.

Democratic party leaders agree that an African-American on the party's ticket would mean not only certain defeat in the presidential contest but the defeat of countless other Democratic candidates for both national and statewide office. And so party leaders and most Democratic primary voters, after the Michigan primary, rally around the most visible and front-running white candidate. Summing the vote for Dukakis and Jackson (in the table, above) makes clear the rapid polarization of voters along the lines of race in the 1988 Democratic presidential primaries.

And Michael Dukakis, as the Democratic party's presidential nominee, proves to have even more vulnerabilities than does George Bush. It's not unreasonable to conclude that, in 1988, Jackson = Dukakis = Bush. The vulnerabilities of George Bush, in 1992, in turn make possible the election to the

White House of a previously unknown Democratic governor from a small state. So Jackson = Dukakis = Bush = Clinton. Why? Racial division in American politics.

That race can be a critical factor in American politics is no surprise, however committed we might be to the principles of equal opportunity for all and equality under the law for all. The significance of race in the politics of each of the fifty states is directly proportional to the prominence of the state's African-American population-- from statistically zero percent in Utah to 40 percent and more in Alabama and Mississippi. Since at least the Civil War, and not only in southern states, lower-class whites have had much to gain and little to lose by identifying their interests with the interests of lower-class blacks, but racial loyalties invariably have superseded class identity. (Which is another reason why a Marxist analysis of American politics is more wrong than right.)

Since the 1960s, whenever a black candidate has opposed a white candidate for the office of mayor of a large city, a sizable majority of white voters usually has voted for the white candidate, but the black candidate has won virtually all the votes cast by black voters. In terms of voting behavior, the African-American electorate is more racially motivated than any other culturally defined voting bloc in American politics. Even when it is in the apparent self-interest of black voters to vote for a liberal white candidate, as in local school board elections, their votes go overwhelmingly to the more conservative school board candidate who is black.

Secessionist movements seeking to incorporate an enclave of a large city are currently organized in Los Angeles, San Francisco, Seattle, Boston, New York City, Miami, Dallas, Memphis, New Haven, Stamford (CT), Portland (ME), and in the District of Columbia. In all these cases the secessionist campaign appears to be driven primarily by race. Nor is this surprising in terms of demographic trends: While 80 percent of

Black, Asian, and Hispanic minorities in the U.S. live in urban metropolitan areas, two-thirds of all white Anglo-Americans live in areas that are at least 90 percent white, typically in the suburbs. And while race is the most important cultural variable explaining patterns of American politics, this still says nothing about the important roles sometimes played by religion and, as currently is the case in California, Texas, Florida and some other states, by language.

So is the United States a "model country of multicultural coexistence"?

Reinforcing Divisions

Answers to controversial questions, of course, are likely to be controversial. Some clarification of the problem may be gained--and so a tentative reduction in the level of controversy, by thinking comparatively. Looking at a variety of countries, what appears to heighten the levels of culture conflict?

The genuine threat of Quebec's separation from the rest of Canada is based on a classic case of reinforcing cultural divisions. Most native French-speaking Canadians are Catholic (and live in Quebec) and most native English-speaking Canadians are Protestant (and live in Canada's other provinces). The prolonged and brutal conflict between Tamil-speaking and Sinhalese-speaking populations in Sri Lanka (Ceylon) is also based on their religious differences: the Tamils are Hindu and the Sinhalese are Buddhist. Less brutal conflict in Belgium, but more prolonged, derives from the conflict between two language groups, Flemish and French, whose opposing attitudes toward the Catholic Church reinforce their language division: Flemish-speaking Belgians are stronger supporters of the Church's involvement in social and political life while the French-speaking Walloons are more hostile to the Church's involvement in secular affairs. Guerrilla insurrection in the Philippines, at various times throughout this century, has been based on native-speaking Filipinos who are Muslim and who oppose the dominance in Manila and on the main islands of Spanish-speaking Christians: the conflict is further reinforced by the unequal distribution of land, to the disadvantage of the Muslims. And the savagery of the conflict in the former Yugoslavia reflects the long-playing animosities of ethnic groups whose reinforcing divisions, with hindsight, seem to have been miraculously subdued during the Communist era.

Cultural divisions along the lines of race, religion, or language may be the basis of social and political conflict, but cultural divisions also may be reinforced by other divisions that are not specifically cultural. The national elections held in the Republic of South Africa, immediately following the end of legal segregation, introduced partisan divisions that reinforced long-standing divisions along the lines of language and tribal identity. In Mexico and in most other Latin American countries, the native Indian populations are socially and economically subordinate to the descendants of Spanish and Portuguese colonizers and to the large mestizo (mixed) populations. Cultural division in Northern Ireland also is reinforced by economic conditions: Catholics typically are employed in lower-skill jobs, are the first to be laid off in bad times and the last to be hired in good times, have lower incomes and inferior housing, and their children are likely to go to Catholic schools. Catholics living in Quebec and in Northern Ireland, and Arabs living in Israel, have their religious differences with the rest of their society reinforced by a whole range of economic and social divisions, and by significant political and ideological differences as well: In Israel, extreme left parties draw most of their support from Israel's Arab population, while Israelis right-wing parties are based on the orthodox and ultra-orthodox faithful of Israel's Jewish majority. Until recently, Flemish-speaking and pro-Church Belgians were more likely to live in rural areas and to be employed in agriculture, while French-speaking and anti-Church Belgians were more likely to live in urban-industrial areas and to be employed in manufacturing and commerce.

Division, of course, is the rule, not the exception. We long ago left behind the unity and homogeneity of social relationships based exclusively on the family, the extended kinship group, and the tribe. Modern society and its characteristic political expression, the nation-state, are inevitably divided by cultural, economic, political and ideological differences. The essential role of government is to negotiate compromises between the society's competing groups in order to keep the inevitable conflicts from erupting into violent confrontation and civil war. This task is all the more difficult as a society's competing groups are set off from each other by multiple divisions, whether cultural, economic or political, that are mutually reinforcing.

Cross-cutting Divisions

The Gallup International polling organization, in the mid-1970s, carried out an ambitious and expensive opinion poll that has never been replicated. Approximately five thousand respondents, drawn mostly from the ranks of corporate executives, judicial elites, and other professionals living in forty different countries, were asked this question: "Omitting your own country, what country of the world do you think is best governed?" The rank-ordered results are as follows:

1. Switzerland	6. United States
2. Great Britain	7. Denmark
3. Sweden	8. Netherlands
4. West Germany	9. Australia
5. Canada	10. Japan

According to Gallup's respondents, what does it take to be a "best governed" country? Political scientists would be quick to note that, of the top ten best governed countries on Gallup's list, nine have a parliamentary form of government; only the

U.S. has a presidential form of government. Five of the ten are unitary states while five are federal states. And all ten countries are among the world's economic elite, in terms of level of development and per capita income. But what does the list tell us about good government and multiculturalism?

Six of the ten best governed countries on Gallup's list are, culturally, overwhelmingly homogeneous. Either there are no significant racial, religious or linguistic minorities among the population, or the country's political and economic development has been almost the exclusive affair of elites drawn from the dominant culture group. The four exceptions, in the order considered below, are West Germany, Canada, Switzerland, and the United States. But we already have some strong evidence, thanks to Gallup International, that cultural homogeneity significantly improves a society's chances of enjoying government that is stable, democratic, and effective.

Religious divisions in West Germany between Catholics and Protestants, after World War II, was immediately reinforced by politics: The dominant Christian Democratic Union, and especially its Bavarian allies, were based on traditional Catholic loyalties while the opposition Social Democrats received their most consistent support from Germany's traditionally Protestant areas (although the support of Protestants in Communist East Germany, a solidly Protestant area, was denied the SPD because of Germany's political division). By the early 1970s, however, the dominant CDU had become as secular as Western Europe's other major political parties, and West Germany's remarkable economic growth had created a large middle-class that cut across West Germany's religious divisions. Where one dividing line in a society cuts across another, identities are less sharply defined, old antagonisms are muted, and a politics of coalition-building and compromise is more easily sustained. In West Germany, in Belgium, in Italy and Spain, and in many other countries of the economically developed world, the emergence of a strong middle-class along with economic growth has helped to strengthen democracy by lowering the intensity of culture conflict. And the economic "class struggle" that Marx celebrated is reduced to political competition thanks to an enlarging economic pie with plenty of pieces to pass around.

Without its relatively high living standards and substantial middle-class, Quebec might long ago have separated from the rest of Canada. There is less to lose when most people don't have much. But as larger numbers enjoy affluence, political adventure threatens a leap into the dark abyss of economic uncertainty. Still, Canada has remained intact, despite the intense pressures created by reinforcing cultural divisions, and largely because of political structure: Federalism does not cut across cultural divisions as does an enlarging middle-class, but federalism does give cultural minorities a genuine sense of political autonomy and control over their own affairs. As a unitary state and regardless of economic conditions, Canada long ago would have fallen to pieces. But as a federal state, Catholic and French-speaking Canadians in Quebec have been able to elect their own provincial government and to control their own schools, police, and courts. If a majority of Quebec voters eventually vote for separation, it would prove only that, in the face of reinforcing cultural divisions, federalism may help but it also may not be enough. Enter Switzerland.

Switzerland's Number One ranking in Gallup's international poll of professional elites from forty countries is especially remarkable, because Switzerland is a potential battle ground of cultural division, division which, since the Protestant Reformation, has been expressed by violence and even civil war (as recently as 1847 during the Sonderbund war, when Catholic cantons attempted to secede from the confederation). But the Catholic-Protestant division of Swiss society is further complicated by language division, primarily between German-speaking and French-speaking Swiss. If these language and religious divisions were reinforcing, as they are in

Canada, then even Switzerland's famous federalism might have failed to keep the confederation intact. But federalism in Switzerland gives local cultural groups significant local autonomy, _and_ Switzerland's cultural divisions are not reinforcing but instead are cross-cutting. The table below helps to underline the point.

Cross-cutting Cultural Divisions in Switzerland

(Total Number of Cantons = 23)

Number of cantons where most people are:	Number of cantons where most people speak:		
	German	French	Italian
Protestant	9	3	-
Catholic	7	3	1

Thus German-speaking Swiss (for example) can identify with both German-speaking Catholics and German-speaking Protestants, while Swiss Protestants can identify with both German-speaking Protestants and French-speaking Protestants. Switzerland, in fact, is the classic example of political and social stability in the context of multi-cultural identities, primarily because cultural identities in Switzerland are not reinforcing.

We may quickly add some other variables that help to moderate cultural tension and conflict because of their cross-cutting effects: monarchy (for example, in Belgium and Spain), a dominant political party (the Christian Democrats in Germany and the Canadian Liberal party), a ruling Communist party (as in the former Yugoslavia, Czechoslovakia, and Soviet Union), the single-member district electoral system (as opposed to a proportional representation electoral system), cross-cultural representation in government (especially at the executive level), a tradition of cooperation and compromise among the leaders of the country's cultural groups and political parties, and neighboring countries that are potentially threatening because they are larger and more powerful.

Which returns us to our initial question: Is the United States a "model country of multicultural coexistence"?

Toward Multicultural Coexistence in the United States?

Federalism in the United States derives from patterns of territorial settlement, both before and after independence from Great Britain. Unlike federalism in Switzerland, then, and federalism in Canada, India, Nigeria, the former Yugoslavia and Soviet Union, and the quasi-federalism more recently instituted in Spain and Belgium, federalism in the United States was not intended and has never functioned as a means to provide specific cultural groups with a sense of political autonomy. The "black power" movement of the 1960s and early 1970s, in part, sought to compensate for this deficiency of American federalism by working to give African-Americans the same control over their own local affairs that had been previously won by those of Scandinavian descent in the upper midwest (especially in Minnesota) and by eastern city Catholics whose families had immigrated from Ireland, Italy, and Central Europe. But African-Americans are geographically too dispersed to be able to develop a culturally-based political autonomy other than occasionally and in a fragmentary way in some major metropolitan areas, such as Detroit, Atlanta, the District of Columbia and Los Angeles, and in various smaller cities and towns in the southern states.

Economic growth and the material affluence of an ever enlarging middle-class, however, has cut across American society's older cultural divisions, especially the religious divisions between Protestants, Catholics, and Jews, and between the various Protestant denominations and sects. Economically driven modernization also tends to moderate religious belief and practice: People still may go to church or temple, but as the commitment to narrow religious dogma declines so does the potential for religious-based conflict. This relationship between modernization and moderating religious belief may be peculiar to only Judao-Christian and, perhaps, Buddhist cultures, because political and social trends in Islamic and Hindu cultures suggest the exact opposite: in these cultures, modernization has fueled a dangerously militant fundamentalism.

Language and especially racial identities, as compared with religious identities, appear to be more resistant to the cross-cutting effects of economic modernization. And, in fact, "melting pot" referred initially and almost exclusively to early America's amalgam of different Protestant denominations. Economic modernization in the U.S. , however, including the "trickling down" fallout from spreading affluence, has created a television-based popular culture and, along with the consequent upward mobility potential for entertainers and professional athletes, this has helped to nourish the growth of an African-American middle class, even the beginnings of a visible African-American upper class.

There also is one significant political institution in the United States that does have the potential for cutting across all the cultural and economic divisions of American society. This is especially ironic because large majorities of opinion poll respondents consistently favor abolishing it: the presidential electoral college.

Because the Constitution requires the winning presidential candidate to capture an absolute majority of electoral votes, and because the electoral votes of each state are distributed according to the principle of winner-take-all, serious contenders for the presidency must build coalitions of voters that are drawn from virtually all the major socioeconomic and cultural groups of American society. Significantly, this mixed mosaic of political clienteles is especially visible in the most populous states where a simple plurality of the popular vote translates into the state's entire treasure chest of electoral votes. Winning pluralities in only California and New York thus gives the candidate almost one-fourth of the electoral vote he needs to move into the White House. No presidential candidate, then, can expect to win if he loses more than two or three of the eight or ten most populous states, and these are precisely the states where the cultural mix is most significant.

So even though Democratic candidates will win the majority of African-American and Hispanic votes, Republican candidates may well depend for victory in a given state on the extent of their minority support from these same cultural groups. This in turn requires presidential candidates and the major political parties to search for ways of appealing to and representing the interests of significant cultural minorities.

Would Colin Powell's name on the Republican national ticket, either as the party's presidential or vice presidential nominee, give the Republicans an advantage in the year 2000? Which is to ask: Would the Republican gain in African-American voters be offset by defecting white voters? Which returns us to the political dynamics set in motion by Jesse Jackson in 1988.

To answer our thematic question about the United States as a model of multicultural coexistence, then, means that we first need to rephrase the question. It is not so much a question of either-or as it is a question of more-or-less. And economic trends and presidential elections will continue to play crucial roles in determining whether it's more or whether it's less.

CHAPTER V

CONFLICT IN MULTICULTURAL SOCIETIES
R. Hrair Dekmejian, Ph.D.*

It may be plausibly argued that conflict rather than coexistence is the predominant mode of behavior in multicultural societies. This negative view of the human condition can be ascertained by a retrospective look at the tragic progression of the 20th Century, with its countless pogroms, deportations, massacres and genocides claiming an estimated total of 170 million lives.[1]

Since primordial times human beings have organized themselves in groups which define their identity and culture. Specific group identities and cultures are formed by shared values resulting from one or a combination of factors: history, tradition, experience, custom, kinship, tribe, religion, race, language, class, region, gender and civilization. Thus, cultures define the identity of social groups and denote the boundaries among them. At the macro-level, cultural identities are manifested in the mosaic of ethnic groups that characterizes the populations of most of the world's nation-states. At the macro-level, the global community is segmented by several overarching cultures and civilizations with diverse values and lifeways.[2]

Although conflicts among ethnocultural groups and civilizations have been endemic since the dawn of history, they have assumed a special salience as a disruptive force in the 20th Century. The global expansion of the European empires and their domination over many non-western societies exposed the latter to Western cultural norms which were imposed upon them in the name of the West's "civilizing mission". The clash among the European imperial states in World

---

*R. Hrair Dekmejian is Professor of Political Science, University of Southern California. He holds a Ph.D. from Columbia University.

War I ended in the defeat of Germany, Austro-Hungary and Ottoman Turkey and the dismemberment of their empires is keeping with US President Woodrow Wilson's call for national self-determination. In the aftermath of World War II, the process of decolonization continued with the dissolution of the remaining European imperial entities. Yet none of the nation-states emerging from the ruins of empire was a socially homogenous entity, but a multiethnic collectivity often held together by state power. Lacking the mechanisms and traditions of multicultural cooperation and coexistence, many of the new states of the Third World have experienced internal conflict among their subgroups, leading to civil unrest, repression and genocide. The Soviet Union's demise and the end of the Cold War ushered in a new phase of intensified ethnocultural conflict within as well as between states, which has caused immense difficulties for the United Nations and the international community.

Ethnocultural Resurgence vs. Globalization

Several divergent social phenomena have characterized the global community in the Cold War's aftermath. Concurrent with the resurgence of ethnocultural movements are the contemporary dynamics of economic globalization and political regionalism. At a time when most of the European states have merged their competing sovereignties into the European Union, a plethora of ethnic groups have sought to pursue their agendas of cultural autonomy and political independence. Meanwhile, indigenous cultures are threatened by the powerful current of socioeconomic globalization which has been defined by Western cultural norms and structural frameworks. These dialectical trends and relationships are at the core of the unfolding panorama of world affairs at the onset of the 21st Century.

In recent decades the West's cultural and political hegemony has been challenged by non-Western cultural traditions that predate the West. This challenge, driven by the rise of indigenization movements, has been viewed with alarm as a "clash of civilizations," a series of *Kulturkampf* between the West and non-Western cultural traditions. Among the alarmists are such prominent thinkers as Professors Samuel Huntington of Harvard and Bernard Lewis of Princeton, who view the incipient civilizational clash as having a detrimental socio-political impact on the West and the world order. Huntington's thesis on the coming clash of civilizations posits the uniqueness of Western Civilization as based on democratic values, the rule of law, separation of spiritual and temporal authority, social pluralism, representative institutions and commitment to individual rights.[3] Because these core features of Western Civilization are not shared globally, there will be an inevitable conflict between the West and its Islamic, Hindu, Confucian, Japanese, Slavic-Orthodox, African and Latin American counterparts.[4] Hence, Huntington's call for Western unity, in order to preserve the integrity of Western civilization.[5]

The clarion call to preserve the West's uniqueness has triggered a wide-ranging debate between Huntington and his detractors. Some of his critics emphasize the possibility of coexistence or osmosis among civilizations, while others seek to maintain the integrity of non-Western civilizations against the West's cultural onslaught and political domination.[6] The latter position in defense on non-Western civilizations has found a vocal advocate in the person of Mahathir Muhammad, the Prime Minister of Malaysia, who has spoken out about the preservation of "Asian values" against the West's cultural imperialism. Even more vocal are exponents of Islamic traditionalism who view with alarm the erosion of the Muslim way of life as a result of the West's cultural penetration of Muslim societies.[7] Thus, the growing trends toward social and economic globalization and the transnational reach of communications media are seen as major threats to the integrity of Islam as a faith and an all-encompassing value system.[8]

Although widely criticized, certain aspects of Huntington's thesis bear relevance to some of the ominous developments in today's world arena. Huntington's supporters can point to the growing confrontation between the West, led by the United States, and the Islamic fundamentalist movement, which has resulted in acts of terrorism and bloodshed. However, the question that begs for an answer is whether this conflict between the West and Islam is triggered by divergent civilizations or by the West's political, economic and cultural hegemony over the Islamic countries. Indeed, it may be plausibly argued that all too often political factors produce cultural and civilizational conflict rather than core cultural differences. Clearly the root causes of intercultural conflict are exceedingly complex, combining a plethora of political, economic, demographic and psychological dimensions which require detailed consideration.

Causal Factors of Ethnocultural Conflict

It is possible to identify at least eight causal factors which generate conflict in multicultural societies. One of the most prevalent is the inferior political status of one ethnocultural group vis-a-vis a dominant group. This condition of political inequality may be the result of conquest or a revolutionary takeover of power by one group to the exclusion of others. A related cause of conflict is the use of state power by the dominant group against a subordinate group, ranging from forced cultural integration to repression, ethnic cleansing and genocide. Still another trigger of conflict is the migration of an ethnic group into the territory of another, escaping repression or economic hardship.

Ethnic conflicts also result from growing numerical imbalances among two or more groups because of population movements or unequal rates of population growth. Even more serious are situations where ethnic groups have competing claims on the same territory or where there exist major disparities of wealth among ethnic groups, which produce class conflicts. No less troublesome are incompatible belief systems between two or more ethnocultural groups which may result in inter-cultural conflict or a clash of civilizations.

Although the foregoing factors, singly or in combination, are potential triggers of interethnic conflict, the role of political elites constitutes a key element in the dynamics of inter-group relations. Competing leaders of ethnocultural groups and national leaders are placed in a key position to exacerbate or resolve conflicts depending on their particular abilities, per-sonality traits or political interests. All too often ethnic and national elites become the catalysts of inter-communal conflict in order to strengthen their hold on power or to further their political careers. A case in point is the Bosnian war triggered, to a large extent, by Yugoslav President Slobodan Milosovic's appeal to Serbian nationalism and Bosnian President Alija Izetbegovic's use of Islam as a mobilizing ideology to rule over a multiethnic state. Thus, both leaders sought to shore up their hold on power by appealing to extremist ideologies which led to bloodshed.[9] Even more tragic were the psychopatholo-gy of Adolf Hitler and the Nazi elite which led to the demo-nization of the Jews and the Holocaust.[10]

Major Conflicts in Multicultural Settings

Conflict in multicultural societies is a pervasive phenomenon in today's global landscape. Most of these conflicts involve disputes between ethnic minorities and nation states. In a pio-neering study, Ted Robert Gurr identified 227 politically active minorities which were at risk during 1945-89, later expanded to include a total of 268 ethnopolitical groups (1990-95).[11]

Although many ethnocultural conflicts develop cyclically, some manifest long-term staying power and protracted vio-lence. These include the Arab-Israeli conflict, Northern Ireland, the Kurdish struggle in Turkey and Iraq, Sudan's civil wars, and the Tutsi vs. Hutu struggle.

The half-century since Israel's independence has been marked by warfare, terrorism and repression. The US-sponsored 1993 Oslo peace process has faltered since 1996, because of Israel's reluctance to withdraw from Arab territories and Palestinian terrorism against Israel.[12] The quest for Palestinian independence and the unsettled status of Jerusalem are issues that transcend Arabs and Israelis to affect the sentiments of Jews, Muslims and Christians the world over. Clearly the unresolved status of Jerusalem and Arab Palestine are at the heart of an escalating global conflict that may be characterized as a "clash of civilizations" between the Islamic world and the United States and Israel.

The conflict in Northern Ireland is rooted in the English conquest of Ireland and centuries of British/Protestant misrule over the Irish Catholic population. When the Irish Republic became independent in 1948, the six northern counties (Ulster) were placed under the British crown, where the Protestant majority ruled over an under-privileged Catholic minority. A peaceful series of Catholic marches inspired by the US civil rights movement were met by Protestant repression and the onset of terrorism by the Irish Republican Army and Protestant militants. The deployment of British troops in 1971 brought an expansion of the IRA's terrorism to Britain and British targets in Europe.[13] After lengthy negotiations under the aegis of the Clinton Administration, Northern Ireland's warring factions signed a power-sharing agreement on Good Friday 1998 to be overseen by the British and Irish governments. This was a promising start along the road to communal peace, although its success or failure will have to await the test of time.

The Kurdish struggle for independence was aborted when the victorious Allies permitted Turkey to renounce the Treaty of Sevres (1920), which had promised to establish an independent Kurdistan. Thus, most of the Kurdish homeland was placed under the reconstituted borders of Turkey, Iraq and Iran.

Repeated Kurdish attempts since the 1920s to secure cultural autonomy and independence have been suppressed in all three countries. In the last decade, the Kurds have been subjected to repeated acts of ethnic cleansing and genocidal massacre, in Turkey and in Iraq under Saddam Hussein. A nation of 20 million, the Kurds remain a stateless minority, at cultural and physical risk of a very high order.[14]

Among Africa's many tribal and sectarian conflicts, the Sudan and Rwanda are paramount in terms of the scale of human suffering and death. Since the Sudan's independence, successive governments led by Arab-Muslim northerners have sought to subjugate the Christian and Animist tribes of the South, with disastrous consequences. The sectarian fighting intensified in 1989, when a military regime took power and established an Islamic theocracy. Thus, the struggle between North and South is not only tribal or ethnic, but a cultural war where the regime is dedicated not only to achieving military victory over the southern tribes but also their conversion to Islam. The civil war between the Islamist regime and the Sudan Peoples Liberation Front has brought mass destruction to the South, including famine and genocide perpetrated by the government's forces.[15]

The causes of the Sudan's human tragedy are similar to the triggers of the Tutsi vs. Hutu struggle, which is rooted in historical disparities of power, exacerbated by colonial rule, incompetent indigenous leaders and tribal enmities. In 1994 the Tutsi-Hutu conflict assumed genocidal proportions, affecting Rwanda, Burundi and the Congo.[16]

The foregoing overview of ongoing interethnic conflicts does not inspire optimism for the future. The 20th Century is often called "The Age of Conflict." A more appropriate label would have been "The Genocidal Century" -- one that opened with the Armenian Massacres, reached a bloody crescendo in the Holocaust, and closed with the atrocities in the Sudan and

Rwanda. These patterns of conflict suggest some conclusions regarding the evolution of multicultural societies at the dawn of the 21st Century:

1. Inter-communal conflict will remain a persistent feature of world politics, since the causal factors that generate such conflict persist as the defining elements of the human condition.
2. Interethnic bloodshed can be prevented only by competent and selfless ethnic and national leaders, combined with timely intervention by international or regional organizations driven by humanitarian considerations and not by narrow state interests.
3. Effective intervention requires a concert among the major powers led by the United States, and acting in the name of an enlightened world community backed by a global popular consensus to make the peaceful resolution of disputes a matter of first priority.
4. Long-term peaceful coexistence among diverse ethnocultural groups requires a restructuring of centralized authoritarian states, in order to promote a high degree of ethnic autonomy and democratic participation in the political process.

NOTES

1. Rudolph J. Rummel, "Power, Genocide and Mass Murder",
Journal of Peace Research, Vol. 31, No. 1, 1994, 4-5.
2. Samuel P. Huntington, "The Clash of Civilizations?"
Foreign Affairs, Vol. 72, No. 3, Summer 1993, 22-29
3. Samuel P. Huntington, "The West Unique, Not Universal,"
Foreign Affairs, Vol. 75, No. 6, November/December 1996, 28-41.
Also see, Bernard Lewis, "The Roots of Muslim Rage,"
The Atlantic Monthly, Vol. 266, September 1990, 60
4. Huntington, "The Clash," 25-49
5. Huntington, "The West Unique, Not Universal," 41-46.
6. See Fouad Ajami, Kishore Mahbubani, Robert Bartley, Liu Binyan,
Jeanne F. Kirkpatrick, "On` The Clash of Civilizations,'"
Foreign Affairs, Vol. 72, No. 4, September/October 1993, 1-26.
Roy P. Mottahedeh, "The Clash of Civilizations: An Islamist's Critique," *Harvard Middle Eastern and Islamic Review*, No. 2, 1996,
1-26; Hayward R. Alker, "If Not Huntigton's `Civilizations,' Then Whose?," *Review*, XVIII, No. 4, Fall 1995, 533-562.
7. R. Hrair Dekmejian, *Islam in Revolution*, 2nd ed. (Syracuse: Syracuse University Press, 1995) 29-32.
8. *Al-Jazira* (Riyadh) July 10, 1998, 18; `*Ukaz* (Jedda)
July 5, 1998, 7.

9. Robin Alison Remington, "Ethnonationalism and the Disintegration of Yugoslavia," in *Global Consulsions*, edited by Winston A. Van Horne (Albany, N.Y.: SUNY Press, 1997) 273-279

10. Robert S. Robins and Jerrold M. Post, *Political Paranoia* (New Haven, Ct.: Yale University Press, 1997) 281-293.

11. Ted Robert Gurr, *Minorities at Risk Phase III Dataset* (College Park, MD: University of Maryland, August 1996).

12. Galia Golan, "Israel and Palestinian Statehood," in *Global Convulsions*, 169-187.

13. Marianne Elliott, "Religion and Identity in Northern Ireland," in *Global Convulsions*, 149-167

14. Yasar Kamel, "The Dark Cloud Over Turkey," *Index of Censorship*, 1, 1995, 141-149; Chris Kutschera, "Kurds in Crisis," *The Middle East*, November 1995, 6-10.

15. William Langewiesche, "Turabi's Law," *The Atlantic Monthly*, August 1994, 20-33.

16. Frank J. Parker, "The Why's in Rwanda," *America*, August 27, 1994, 6-9.

Index